YANIA TIERRA

A Documentary Poem

Aída Cartagena Portalatín

YANIA TIERRA

Poema documento — Document Poem

by Aída Cartagena Portalatín

Introduction & Notes
by M.J. Fenwick

Translated
by M.J. Fenwick
& Rosabelle White

A Critical Bilingual Edition

Azul Editions
MCMXCV

Copyright © 1982 Aída Cartagena Portalatín
Bilingual Edition Copyright © 1995 Azul Editions
Translation Copyright © M.J. Fenwick
All rights reserved

No part of this book may be reproduced
by any means in any form without the written
permission of the publisher

Published by
Azul Editions
2032 Belmont Road, N.W.
Suite 301
Washington, D.C. 20009
USA

ISBN 0-9632363-9-3
Library of Congress Catalog Number: 94-79182

Printed in the United States of America

First Edition
10 9 8 7 6 5 4 3 2 1

CONTENTS

Introduction   11

Yania Tierra   30

Notes   175

Bibliography   187

Historical References   189

ACKNOWLEDGMENTS

I met Aída Cartagena Portalatín in Santo Domingo in the summer of 1990 at the annual conference of the Association of Caribbean Studies. She asked me, as a university professor in the United States, to do something to help inform the people of my country about the Dominican Republic, its literature and its history — to help disperse Dominican books to our university libraries and to include Dominican literature in our seminars. This bilingual edition of *Yania Tierra* was born from her impassioned plea that day. We are indebted to The University of Memphis for its support of the project, to Elizabeth Buck of the University Interlibrary Loan Department, DeAnna Williams and Rosabelle White, graduate students in the Department of Foreign Languages and Literatures, and to Ursula Schott-Pujol and María Isabel Schott Read from Santo Domingo for their research and translation assistance and to Thomas Collins, of the *Santa Fe Reporter*, for his editorial assistance.

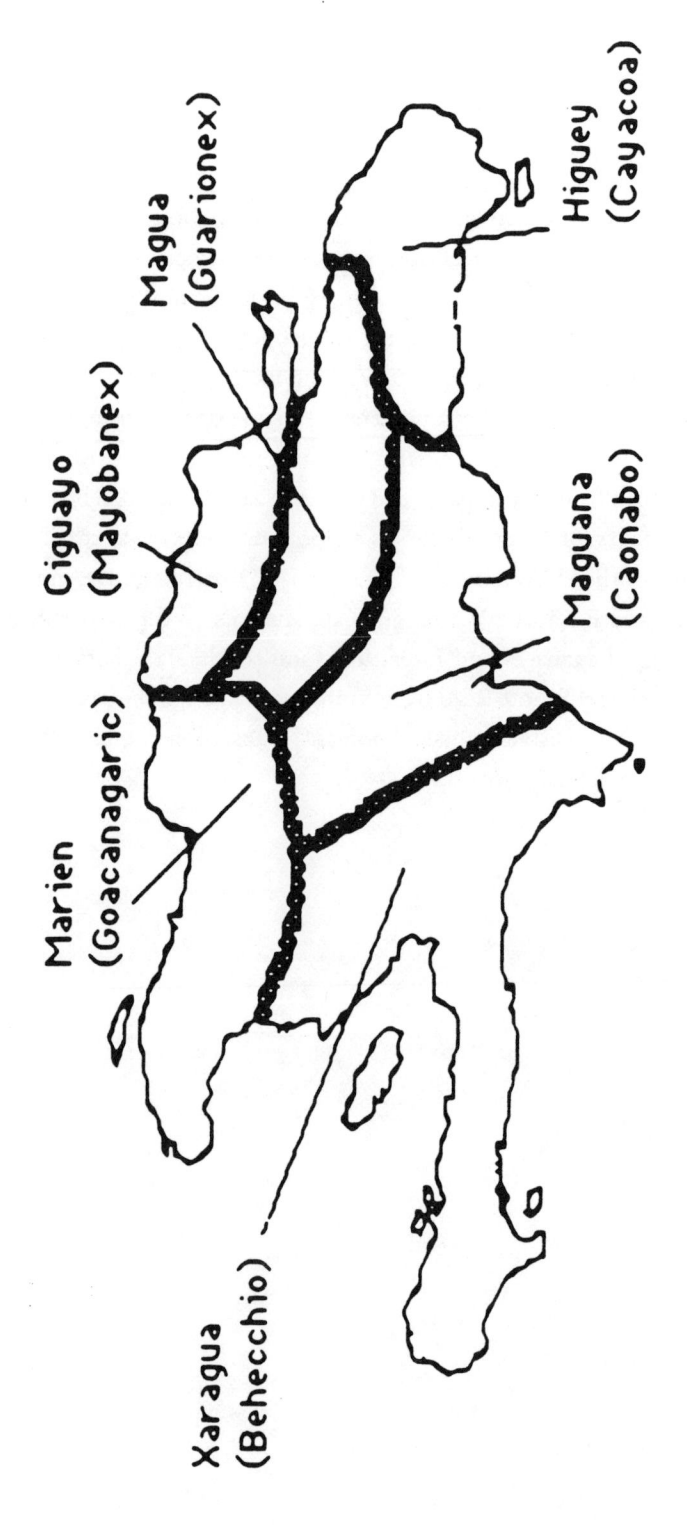

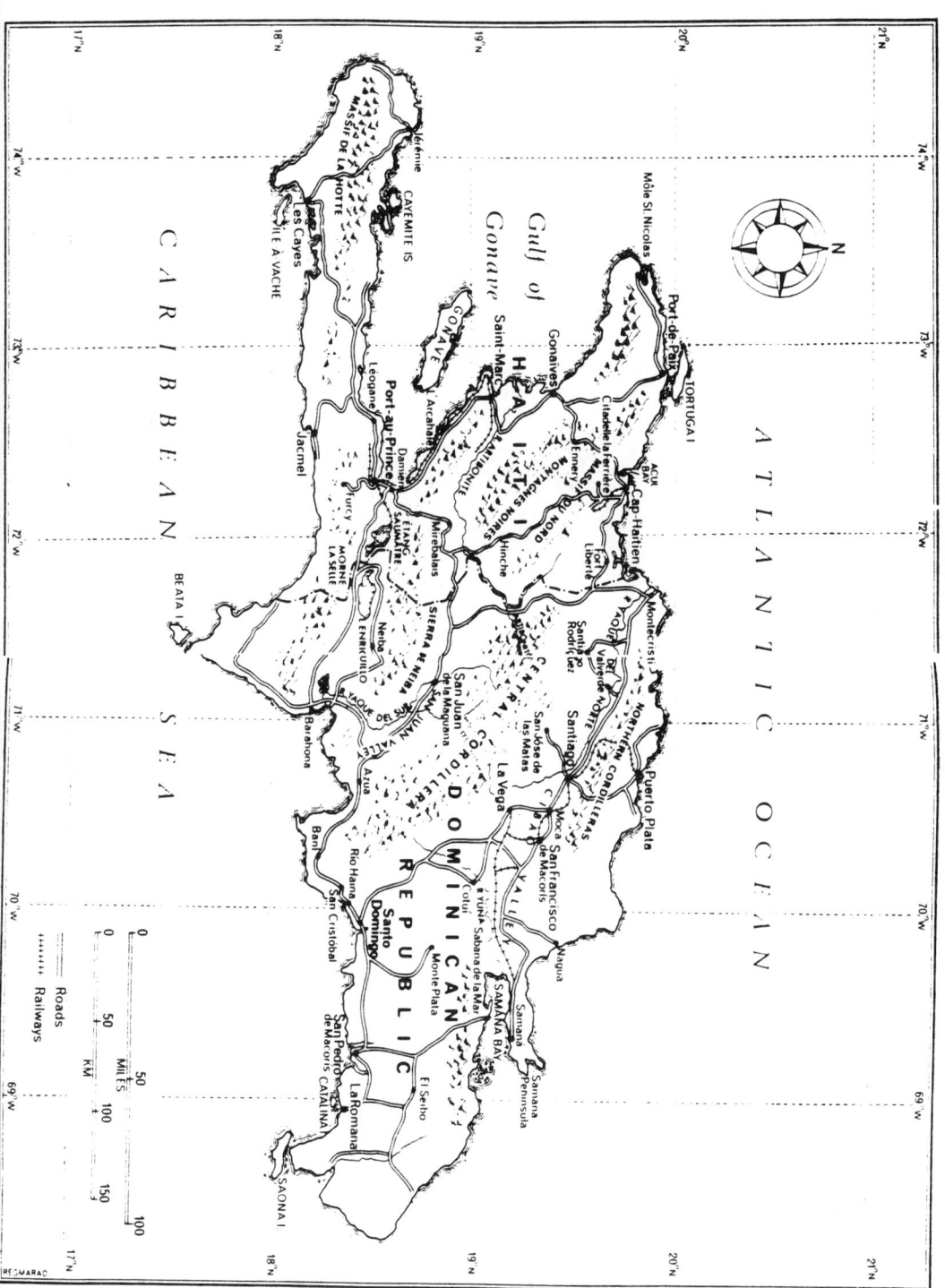

INTRODUCTION

The Dominican Republic is the eastern part of the island that Christopher Columbus named Hispaniola, the second largest island in the Caribbean once inhabited by people who called themselves the Taíno, a culture formed from the historical synthesis of several ancient societies which had migrated over centuries from South and Central America. The Taíno on Hispaniola were distinguished as six separate chiefdoms that shared the island in relative comfort and peace. The population of the Taíno society is estimated to have reached over a half million in their final century with an economy based in agriculture, fishing, hunting and trade with other societies in the Caribbean region. However, history as the Taíno had known it came to an end in 1492 when Columbus landed in the chiefdom of Marién on the northwest coast the Taíno's homeland and, in his medieval European enthnocentricity, claimed it in the name of the Spanish Crown which had funded his voyage. From this date, Columbus began to document the historic encounter between the Taíno and the Spanish in his own terms and to record his impressions of the conquered lands and peoples — in effect, to rewrite their history. At the end of more than 300 years of colonial domination in 1844, the writers of the Dominican Republic began an attempt to recover the stories of their indigenous past and document history from the perspective of the Taíno. Although few modern Dominicans shared a racial or ethnic relationship with the ancient Taíno society, many post-colonial Dominican writers looked to the Taíno heritage as a symbolic historical connection shared by virtue of their common homeland and their struggles for self-determination.

Aída Cartagena Portalatín was a writer from this tradition. She was a short story writer, poet, novelist, literary critic, feminist scholar and educator. Her life spanned the twentieth century, and her work projected the aspirations of her people throughout. She was a remarkable woman who dedicated her life and literary career to raising political consciousness about her country and its historical struggles. Not only did the content of her work bear an explicit historical design, but also the independent form of her literary expression was consistent with the particular cultural experience that inspired her work. Her career as one of the most important writers in Latin America and the Caribbean ended with her recent death in 1994, but her work remains as an important challenge to us throughout the Americas to read and to act politically.

Yania Tierra, originally published in 1981, is a documentary poem about the history of the Dominican Republic. The narrative of the poem traces the continuous exploitation of the nation, its people and its wealth for 500 years by foreign powers, beginning with the confrontation between the indigenous people and Christopher Columbus on December 25, 1492, continuing through the centuries of conquest and colonization by the Spanish, later incursions by the French, English and Dutch, multiple invasions by Haiti, continuous struggles for Independence until the victory of 1844, the difficult Restoration period, and concluding with a century of dictatorships and interference by the United States. In addition to its historical purpose, *Yania Tierra* is also a declaration of a new kind of poetry whose artistic free form symbolically corresponds to the dynamics established through its images — flow of dates, popular struggles and heroes — and their trajectory through the 82 pages of the poem. The dominant images in the poem are of women and their participation in the heroic struggles. The Dominican Republic, or Hispaniola, was the first to suffer the brutal impact of conquest and full colonization and, in many ways, serves as a paradigm for Caribbean colonial history.

Yania Tierra (Yania López) is the protagonist of the poem, a female personification of Hispaniola and the Dominican nation, both a victim and a relentless hero, "All Yania branded and enslaved / By giant possessive rivals." (35) The central action of the poem is Yania's march, like a funeral procession across the land and through time, the five centuries of exploitation. Other protagonists are Yania's loyal supporters who walk with her, represented by a figure called the cripple (el cojito) through whose eyes we accompany Yania and understand her plight. Another protagonist is a figure called the idiot (el tonto) who is upset by the historical events but stands around cracking his knuckles, unable to act in any meaningful way. Both the cripple and the idiot are symbolic images of two kinds of Dominican citizens: those who are loyal but powerless to change her course (the cripple) and those who are easily distracted by insignificant things to change her course (the idiot). The two figures suggest a class identity or at least a political consciousness: the cripple, who knows the historical struggles by memory, seems to represent the oppressed rural and urban working sectors; and the idiot seems to represent the idle patriot whose political consciousness is limited to silly fretful gestures. The reader is pulled into the poem as witness to Yania and her story. Along the way, as Yania marches through history, we get a close look at both the villains and the heroic women who played important parts in the continuous struggles against exploitation. The villains and heroes are represented not by symbolic images but by their real names.

The first time period revealed in the poem is the Conquest. The idyllic setting of indigenous America is counterposed with the sudden and violent intrusion of the conquerors whose wealth was to be made from gold, sugar and hides exported to Spain and eventually to other European nations. "Now Peace sees helmets and lances / Dominate present and future scenes." (47) We witness the indigenous caciques, Anacaona and her court of virgins reduced to slavery to serve the Spanish conquerors, provide their food supply, construct their fortresses and houses, and work the rivers and mines for gold. Anacaona was cacique of Jaraguá, one of the six chiefdoms of the Taíno. The importance of women in the Dominican struggle is established with Chief / Queen Anacaona who led a heroic rebellion against the invaders. Although the rebellion was unsuccessful, Anacaona's efforts are legendary in Dominican historical consciousness. She and thousands of Taíno people were exterminated under the command of Nicolás de Ovando, the Governor of Hispaniola and official representative of the Spanish Crown from 1502 to 1509. The poem documents other villains and heroes from the conquest and colonization period in Hispaniola. The Vicereine María de Toledo, the wife of Viceroy Diego Colón, was known for her compassion toward the indigenous citizens and respect for the integrity of their culture. Leonor de Ovando, Mother Prioress and the first woman poet of Hispaniola, and Elvira de Mendoza, also a poet, were colonial heroes from popularized historical accounts.

Gold was the primary commodity to the new post-feudal Spanish economy and was entirely dependent on indigenous labor. A system of repartimientos and encomiendas was established to distribute the indigenous citizens among the colonizers to work the land and mines for them. This labor was essential to the riches shared by the colonizers; but, by most accounts, within thirty years no more than 1% of the indigenous population was still alive. They were exterminated through combat, abusive labor conditions, malnutrition and disease. As a result, mining diminished; and, without the possibility of accumulated wealth from gold mines, colonizers began to leave Hispaniola. From the 10,000 during the early boom years, the population of colonizers fell to less than 1,000 by 1516. Soon, however, the colonial economy of Hispaniola was rescued by African slaves imported as early as 1517 to replace the diminished indigenous labor force, necessary to prop up the exploitation process. The economic base was changed to sugar, and the Africans constructed and worked in the new sugar mills and in the production of meat and hides. Sugar production revived the colonial economy of Hispaniola. It was first exported in 1521; and, as African slave trade increased, by 1527 sugar became essential to the colonial economic base throughout the Caribbean. By 1548 there were 35 sugar plantations in operation in Hispaniola alone. Sugar production for export reached its peak in 1603. "YANIA watches / Sugar mills are erected / her womb is penetrated / Gold is washed / For the kingdoms of Western Europe / The black man exploited like a beast." (79)

The enormous wealth extracted during the early years of conquest and colonization made Hispaniola the political and cultural center of the Americas. The first bishoprics were located there in 1508, the first royal court in 1510, and the first university in 1538. The new capital city, Santo Domingo, served as the base for exploits to the rest of the Caribbean and Latin America and was a vital colonial port through which most of the early traffic passed. But the colonial cycle of "boom and bust" had already been set in motion. "HE abandons her like that / naked / Her sheet ripped / Under an open sky." (37)

Gold and profits from sugar and hides were officially held by Spanish monopoly control. All legal trade was required to pass through the Spanish port of Sevilla, but the rich colonial market was coveted by contending European powers, the British, the French and the Dutch. Beginning around 1538, all the Spanish Antilles were threatened by pirates and corsair invasions, an activity which plagued the Caribbean for another two hundred years. In 1562, British merchant sailor John Hawkins, backed by financial investors interested in marketing slaves for sugar, hides and wood, landed in the old port of Isabela on the north coast with a cargo of slaves and set up business. "In Old Isabela he directs the exchange / of hides / of sugar / For the miserable merchandise of black / slaves." (77) In 1586, the British adventurer Francis Drake and his crew, supported by Queen Elizabeth I, landed on the north coast of Hispaniola, marched into Santo Domingo and sacked the colonial capital, "Rapes / destroys the Colonial City / Redirects its history / in exchange / for a millionaire's sum." (77) Drake abandoned the city only after lengthy negotiations in which the city residents pooled their personal resources of gold, silver and jewelry to compensate him along with other valuables which he took from the cathedrals, the fortress and the storage houses.

After Spain's maritime defeat in 1588 by England, also commanded by Francis Drake, the Spanish colonial monopoly was weakened and British merchant seamen began to do successful business in the colonies. Because Santo Domingo was a Spanish stronghold and strictly bound to the terms of monopoly, ships from the other European nations began to bypass that port for other more receptive and very lucrative markets on the north and west coasts of Hispaniola and elsewhere in the Caribbean. Disloyal Spanish colonists and large communities of free blacks, all eager to escape the high taxes and other profit limitations of the Spanish monopoly bureaucracy, made commercial alliances with the European merchants. Soon Puerto Plata on Hispaniola's north coast came under British control, and Santo Domingo began to decline. In 1605, Governor Antonio de Osorio, acting on orders from the King of Spain, sent troops to the north coast to burn the houses, ranches, churches and crops in an attempt to prevent anyone from benefiting from the contraband with foreign merchants and to bring the northern wealth back to Santo Domingo. Instead of eliminating contraband and recovering the wealth for Hispaniola, Osorio's action caused the reverse. Most citizens sold their cattle and left Hispaniola for nearby Cuba and other islands. His action depopulated the north coast of Hispaniola, destroyed the livelihood of many free mulattos and blacks, destroyed the cattle industry for all of Hispaniola, and cut off the supply of foreign goods which, although illegal, managed to reach and benefit the residents of Santo Domingo, "In the year 5 of 600 the ships change / their routes / over the oceans / bringing more / destruction / death / depopulation / to Hispaniola." (83) All this was done to serve the Spanish Crown monopoly which had all but abandoned service to Hispaniola, and it left the Spanish colony without an industrial base and completely dependent on the ineffectual Spanish monopoly and outside the competitive forces of European commerce. Hispaniola's former economic importance was replaced by Cuba and Puerto Rico by the end of the 1600s.

Other economic disasters plagued Hispaniola in that century. Disease and abuse took a continuous and heavy toll on Hispaniola's population of slaves, and the dependence on slave labor made economic stability precarious. Cacao was expected to be important for Hispaniola's economy after 1650, and the Spanish Crown imported more African slaves to replace those who died in a 1651 epidemic. However, more slaves were killed in 1666 by a smallpox epidemic. A cacao disease in 1666, another epidemic in 1669, a cyclone in 1672 and an earthquake in 1673 further reduced the potential success of cacao production. When finally a boatload of 400 slaves arrived in Santo Domingo, the colonists could only afford to buy a few of them, and the cargo was sent on to other more prosperous ports.

In addition to its dependency on slavery, the colonial plantation economy of Hispaniola was dependent on a strong mercantile system of shipping and trade. Spanish ships were ignoring Santo Domingo, bypassing it for more active and profitable ports in Mexico and Peru. Meanwhile, throughout the 17th century, continued threats to Santo Domingo's economic position came from the success and rapid growth of French settlements, founded by corsairs around 1630 in the northwestern part of Hispaniola. Their success was due to the heavy import of slaves supported by French commercial interests whereby the production of sugar and tobacco was kept stable. Their desire for economic and territorial expansion was a source of constant conflict between the two populations for control of the whole island. Disputes continued until the new border was finally established in 1777, dividing Hispaniola into two separate colonies, one Spanish and one French. "She an Island one day divided down the middle / Boundaries changing in all the mirrors / Like the frames in an old / Movie projector." (65)

The turn of the 19th century and the chaotic decades leading to national independence are well elaborated in the poem. The French Revolution in 1789, which overthrew the monarchy and abolished slavery in the French colonies, had an important impact on all of Hispaniola. War between Spain and France and two centuries of serious economic difficulties for Spain resulted in a treaty signed in 1795 which ceded the remaining impoverished Spanish colony in Hispaniola to the French. Meanwhile, in the western part of Hispaniola, an incipient bourgeoisie of slave owning colonists, both white and free mulatto, was struggling against a population of mulatto and black slaves which significantly outnumbered them. The success of the French Revolution inspired revolts on all the plantations, and former slave Toussaint L'Ouverture emerged in 1800 as the governor and commander-in-chief of the army. His campaigns to organize former slaves against the landowners and establish an egalitarian society caused most of the former landowners to leave for Cuba where slavery was still intact. In France, post revolutionary emperor Napoleon Bonaparte had begun a campaign to maintain his colonial possessions. Toussaint L'Ouverture, anticipating the power struggle, invaded Santo Domingo in 1801 with the purpose of uniting both parts of the island and defending Hispaniola from Napoleon's expansion. He also sought to free the slaves in Santo Domingo, but this perhaps heroic act was seen by the Dominicans as another act of aggression since for some time their economic position had precluded maintaining slaves. The Dominicans successfully resisted Toussaint L'Ouverture but faced half a century of further invasions and occupations by the Haitians.

Four years later, in 1805, the year after Haiti had gained full independence from France, the new Haitian emperor-self-proclaimed, Jean-Jacques Dessalines, invaded Santo Domingo again. In 1809, Santo Domingo managed to free itself a second time from Haitian rule and anticipated joining the other Spanish colonies in Latin America in preparing for independence from Spain which was finally achieved in 1821 only to be invaded a third time by Haiti's president, General Jean-Pierre Boyer and his troops. This occupation lasted until 1844, "YEARS of Boyer / Herard / Borgellá and Carrié / Scum of the scum / A horizon without hope / The tam-tam of drums from the West." (85) The half century of Haitian invasions is portrayed in the poem by images of rape and murder against Yania and her women. Yania, of course, is symbolic, but the women, the villains and the events are from actual history. Boyer, Herard, Borgellá and Carrié were Haitian, all leaders — presidents and generals — who followed the tradition set by the colonial oppressors and led the invasions against the Dominican nation. The women named in the poem were brave women who, in one capacity or another, took a heroic stand against the invader, and many were killed. The three Andújar sisters, for example, were innocent young women who were raped and murdered because of their father's participation in the resistance against Haitian troops in 1822 and the subsequent wave of terror. "Dishonored virgins / Raped by madness / Murdered / Oh / total damnation / The troops advance from every quadrant / Of Yania's land." (87)

The poem continues through the 19th century tracing the heroic participation of women in the 1844 Independence movement and the numerous struggles that followed to maintain national self-determination. At this point in the poem, the images and poetic rhythm acquire an energetic and victorious dynamic as the names of women are introduced and interwoven with the revolutionary action, all at a very fast-moving pace which simulates the historical events. These women include teachers, writers, actresses, women of high society, wives and lovers of military leaders, and peasant women. Through the activities of women like Concepción Bona and the Villa sisters who sewed the first Dominican flags, Petronila Gau, Juana Saltitopa, María Baltazara de los Reyes and Rosa Montás who armed themselves as revolutionaries in battle, Micaela Rivera who sold her land and possessions for the purchase of war ships and, with her daughter Froilana Febles, made ammunition for the revolutionaries, women of society like Ana Valverde who offered her money and collected from other wealthy women to pay for the repair of the old colonial city wall for the purpose of protecting Santo Domingo from Haitian attacks and María Trinidad Sánchez who carried gunpowder in her skirt during the heat of battle and was later hanged for her revolutionary activity, the poem documents important details of the struggle for national independence. The women of the Philanthropic Society are also important to the poem's development as they were to the 1844 Independence movement. The Society was established ostensibly for literary and entertainment purposes, but their theatre presentations were designed to awaken the passive patriotism of the people and maintain their enthusiasm for national independence, "Inspire in the spectators an overwhelming passion / to win back the land / they have dreamed free." (91)

A woman named Rosa Duarte is central to this section of the poem. Rosa, along with her brother Juan Pablo, their mother and sisters were all leaders and heroes in the 1844 Independence movement. Juan Pablo Duarte was a philosopher and teacher who formulated the manifesto of independence for the Dominican people and was one of the founders of the revolutionary Trinitarian Society. Rosa Duarte was extraordinary, not only for her revolutionary sacrifices but also for her excellent documentation of this important historical moment. The pace of the poem here is quick, powerful and enthusiastic about the Duarte family, the Trinitarian women and the Febrerista women, their participation and leadership in the events surrounding the declaration of national independence in Santo Domingo on the night of February 27, 1844, the declaration of the Republic, free finally from status as a Spanish colony and free from Haitian domination.

Although the 1844 struggle for independence was successful, the period following was filled with economic difficulties and with internal conflicts for power. The new Dominican Republic was essentially bankrupt from the decades of war and faced further aggressions from Haiti. In 1859, the newly-elected President, General Pedro Santana who had been heroic in the 1844 campaign for independence, shocked the sovereign people with his annexation plan to return the Dominican Republic to Spanish colonial status in exchange for Spain's aid during the difficult times, "the selling of the Nation / by Santana." (131) In spite of the massive heroic opposition by Dominicans like poet Cleofes Valdez de Mota who was shot for her opposition to annexation, the Dominican Republic was annexed to Spain from 1861 to 1865, and Spanish troops occupied the country during the last two and a half years called the War for Restoration.

The period after 1865 produced great advances in education and the intellectual emancipation of Dominican women. Women of this historical period like Socorro Sánchez and poet Salomé Ureña de Henríquez are among the first militant feminists, dedicated to the education of women as they were to restoring Dominican constitutional sovereignty. The poem documents these and other educators who founded schools for women and served as the inspiration for future generations of women, undaunted by the almost continuous economic and political instability.

When General Ulises Heureaux, nicknamed Lilís, came to power in 1882, he contracted loans from England, the United States, Germany, Italy, the Netherlands and France. As was usual for Latin American nations in this stage of their development, the interest rate for the loans was very high, and the economic base was insufficient to pay off the loans by the schedule and terms of the contracts. Forced, then, into making further loans to consolidate its debts, the new Dominican Republic soon found itself in an irreversible debt obligation to external powers. Lilís commanded an oppressive regime which enriched him and his friends and impoverished the national government. When Lilís was assassinated in 1899, another revolution ensued with the priority of establishing a leadership which could manage the new national debt.

The next few years were characterized by political unrest in the face of serious economic depression, and the attitude of U.S. foreign policy toward its Latin American debtors was impatient and forceful.

Throughout the Caribbean and Latin America these debts with the U.S. were often used to justify economic and political supervision and sometimes military interference. And so it was for the Dominican Republic. Any sign of instability was used as a pretext for sending troops to protect U.S. interests, all in the name of the Monroe Doctrine revived in the 20th century by President Theodore Roosevelt. There was a rapid succession of Dominican presidents in the years following Lilís' assassination and as many uprisings against the ineffectual political leadership. The U.S. took immediate steps to oversee the collection of its debt. In 1905, U.S. ships came into port at Santo Domingo and took over the administration of Dominican customs. In 1907 the Dominican Republic was put in financial receivership. In 1916, when Santo Domingo was in the hands of anti-U.S. revolutionary forces, the U.S. marines landed in Puerto Plata on the north coast and advanced across the nation to eventually occupy eight of the twelve provinces. U.S. President Woodrow Wilson proceeded to install a U.S.-controlled military government which was in power until 1924, "The Memphis / the marines / The cruel boot of the gringo / The eagle and its rapacious power." (149) During these years, the Dominican Constitution was suspended, U.S. forces occupied the National Palace, the U.S. flag was raised alongside the Dominican flag, censorship was imposed on the national press, and the existing national militia, the national army and the urban police were replaced by a national rural police force under the direction of U.S. officials. Women, again during this period, lived up to the tradition established in the previous centuries. The poem documents the heroic resistance of Ercilia Pepín and Rosa Sméster, educators, feminists, and revolutionaries who steadily fought against U.S. intervention in Dominican internal affairs and guerrilleras Casilda Crespo and Secundina Reyes. Casilda Crespo fought against the U.S. troops in the siege of "Los Come Burros" in 1916 and Secundina Reyes fought in the famous peasant uprisings against U.S. troops in the eastern region of the Dominican Republic where agricultural land was being claimed for U.S. corporations.

One of the most devastating periods in Dominican history was the 31-year dictatorship of Rafael Trujillo and his puppets from 1930 to 1961. Trujillo had been the head of the U.S.-imposed national police force during the eight-year occupation and head of the Dominican national army when it was reinstated in 1924. As dictator, Trujillo maintained close relations with the U.S. through the influence of his former U.S. Marine colleagues and granted the U.S. privileged access to Dominican sugar production. At the same time, Trujillo established a severely repressive totalitarian regime with the Dominican national army at his personal service, and he amassed enormous wealth by appropriating agricultural and industrial enterprises and corporations dealing in foreign trade. It is estimated that finally he had personal control of over 65 percent of the entire national wealth. The poem documents several resistance struggles against Trujillo which gained momentum after World War II. In June 1949, six small planes carrying Latin American revolutionaries united by anti-totalitarian political motives left from Guatemala en route to Luperón on the north coast of the Dominican Republic. Only one plane of the six reached the destination, and its occupants were captured. In 1959, a series of three revolutionary invasions known as the June 14th Clandestine Movement led by worker and student groups landed in Constanza, Maimón and Estero Hondo on the north and east coasts, motivated by the same historical events that inspired the successful Cuban Revolution commanded by Fidel Castro against Fulgencio Batista. Unfortunately, the Dominican invasions were poorly planned and failed with significant numbers of revolutionaries imprisoned or killed. The images of militant women continue to be strong in this section of the poem. The Mirabal sisters, Minerva, Patria and María Teresa, were political activists and feminists who fought along with their spouses in the 1959 Clandestine Movement and were murdered in 1960 by Trujillo's Military Intelligence Service. Minerva was an attorney and theoretical advisor in the 1959 resistance. "The Mirabal sisters were there / Each breast burning with / the pain / the cross / Their eyes a stream of blood / Tears from so many bones / Ashes from so many dead rolled / Down their three faces." (153) Guillermina Puigsubirá (157) was the mother of a revolutionary killed in the June 14th Clandestine Movement. She is important to the testimony because she dedicated the rest of her life gathering the historical information surrounding the events and keeping the heroic memory alive.

The long series of attempts to overthrow the Trujillo dictatorship ended in 1961 with his assassination which, evidence suggests, was directed by the C.I.A. working with internal forces, each with very different motives. For some time the U.S. government had balanced its privileged access to Dominican sugar production against its concern for democracy, but Trujillo's flagrantly anti-democratic activities had become an embarrassment to the official U.S. policy of protecting freedom and democracy for its American neighbors. Also, Trujillo's death offered the U.S. investors the opportunity to buy much of the Trujillo-owned industry and land and, thus, avoid further difficult and compromising negotiations. The U.S. military was subsequently installed to guarantee political stability and profits for the new investors. Clearly, it was important to foreign investors to recover the losses suffered with the success of the Cuban Revolution as there were enormous profits to be made from the Dominican Republic as a source of raw materials, cheap labor, markets for foreign goods and services, strategic military bases and opportunities for influence in regional and international political organizations.

In February of 1963, Juan Bosch was inaugurated as the first democratically elected president since 1924. Bosch's popularity was based on his opposition to the U.S. government's long-standing involvement in the internal affairs of the Dominican Republic and its collaboration with exploitative foreign investments. He was also elected on his promise to redistribute Trujillo-owned land to farmers, to diversify agriculture, to reduce unemployment, guarantee benefits and equitable salaries for workers and to reestablish democratic rights for labor unions and all political parties. In September of 1963, less than eight months after his inauguration, Bosch was ousted by a military coup which evidence strongly suggests was organized by powers within the U.S. government for the purpose of restoring free market advantages for U.S. sugar, oil and mining interests. The poem makes reference to important dates in resistance activities which, together, trace the recent history of the Dominican Republic, "La Manacla — December 23 year 63 / Revolution of April — 24 of 65 / Caracoles — February 6 of 73." (157) After the Bosch ouster in September, an insurrection in the manner of the 1959 Clandestine Movement began on several fronts, but this time the movement was infiltrated and several of the leaders were sent into an ambush at La Manacla and killed. News was received of their death on December 23, 1963. Widespread unrest, labor strikes and anti-U.S. protests continued throughout 1964. On April 24, 1965, another popular revolution began with the purpose of overthrowing U.S.-backed President Donald Reid Cabral and restoring the 1963 Constitution. A small group of revolutionaries seized control of Radio Santo Domingo and called the people into the streets. Immediately, the U.S. Marines invaded under the command of President Lyndon Johnson, supported by a neo-Trujillo bourgeoisie and its military. This time there can be no doubt about their alliance with Texas- and New England-based oil and sugar conglomerates. The people armed themselves with machetes, sticks and guns and fought in the streets against the enemy's tanks and helicopters, "The yankeehoard returns / Settles down on Yania / Three million say NO." (161) Reid Cabral was exiled to Miami, but the U.S. Marines stayed to oversee the 1966 election of President Joaquín Balaguer, a close associate of Trujillo. The last revolutionary attempt mentioned in the poem was at Caracoles in the Bay of Ocoa on the south coast, east of Santo Domingo, on February 6, 1973. This unsuccessful guerrilla-style invasion was headed by Francisco Caamaño who had been involved in the 1965 coup. "Stories come like births / They come / With an aroma of sour placenta / They keep coming from the North / The pirates loot / Riches from coffee / sugar / cacao / gold / silver / nickel / bauxite." (171)

Women again are important in this period documented by the poem. Yolanda Guzmán was a neighborhood organizer killed for her involvement in the April 1965 Revolution, Florinda Soriano, immortalized in popular songs as Mamá Tingó, was a campesina shot for resisting the government's takeover of their land in Yamasá, Hilda Gautreaux was a lawyer who was killed for demanding justice, Amelia Ricart Calventi was killed in 1966 by the National Police during a student protest demanding funds for the University, and María Victoria de la Cruz, known as Doña Chucha, converted her house into a home for abandoned and orphaned children during this revolutionary period. These women from the contemporary generation complete the picture in the Dominican testimony.

The poem's real images of heroic women throughout the poem represent a cross-section of Dominican society, and they span the centuries of invasion and exploitation by foreign powers. Although their class distinctions seem to be forgiven in the poem, the women represent an important political force by virtue of a shared anti-imperialist consciousness. Furthermore, the many women of social privilege, as documented in the poem, are willing to betray their class interests and stand against those Dominican sectors politically aligned with foreign interests which would compromise national self-determination in all its political and economic contexts. The poem's real images of heroes, villains and historical events are connected by the symbolic image of Yania Tierra, the female personification of Hispaniola and the Dominican nation exploited throughout the 500 years since the arrival of the first Europeans.

The poem's literary form does not obey any of the canonized traditions, but its exposition and rhythm are carefully constructed to correspond to the movement of Dominican history. During the moments of revolutionary or resistance activity, the poem's pace increases. Its off-set lines produce the effect of multiple voices echoing and reinforcing the images. The frequent interjections by the cripple offer historical observations and summary. These elements along with the continuous interaction of symbolic images and real historical images do not allow the poem to be reduced to a sentimental, nationalistic romanticism. On the contrary, its literary dynamics demand that the poem be taken as a living testimony to motivate the reader to an active understanding of this 500-year series of events. The poem projects confidence in the historical process driven by the collective struggles of women and men, "Only the inevitable will bring glory / Naked / relentless / in its unchanging course," (35) but parodies that history which has been imposed from the outside by outside interests, "With history begins the fatal oppression / Layer upon layer of gray dirt / Hunger in the slums / Towns and cities / Symmetry of misery." (81)

Finally, beyond its other important contributions, what makes *Yania Tierra* an exceptional work is its focus on the active role of women in history. After eighty-two pages and the stories of more than a hundred heroic women, the poem's last lines are a call to contemporary Dominican women to carry on the struggle.

— M. J. Fenwick
1994

WITH THIS DOCUMENT — POEM
we pay HOMAGE
to the women of our land
who over a period of
five centuries have been murdered
or have sacrificed themselves for their people.

Without the careful researching
of texts by knowledgeable historians
YANIA TIERRA
would probably not exist.

"Modern literature is offered
as a response to the hunger problems
of this world.
The hunger of modern literature
is our immemorial hunger."

". . . when we have written we
feel unsatisfied because that which
remains unwritten is greater
than that which has been written."

— *Carlos Fuentes*
University of Puerto Rico
January 1981

> *"voime a morir*
> *de amor de pena*
> *por no haber visto*
> *otra manera."*

CIERTO / Perdí el viejo juego de los versos
Deseo conversar de otra manera
        cuando la Zarza Ardiente
Se quebranta bajo continuos aguaceros
Con todo el dolor de
        una muerte concebida
Quién sería como Dios en la tierra
Para soportar tanto silencio
Si los testigos de estas letras nuevas
Desean secuestrar la libertad de la palabra
        cotidiana
Que traspasa tu cuerpo Yania Tierra

Nunca mis nuevas voces serán yedra
Asidas a un muro horadando desesperadamente

"i'm gonna die
of sorrow
because i haven't seen
any other way."

IT IS TRUE / I've lost the old rhyming game
I wish to speak in another way
      while the Burning Bush
Is breaking under continuous rainshowers
With all the anguish
      of a death foretold
Who could be like God on earth
Able to bear so much silence
If those who are witness to these new lyrics
Wish to take away the freedom of everyday
      language
That is heard across your body Yania Tierra

Never will my new lyrics be like ivy
Rooted in a wall desperately penetrating

CON este conversar digo amor
Comportamiento compartido
Digo Hombre

    La voz cubre el espacio
Crece / traspasa los bosques
Atascados de sangre los ríos

CON LAS MISMAS PALABRAS DIGO DIOS
LO ENCUENTRO TODO ENTERO

Por las calles y plazas
El bien y el amor
Traspasan las Montañas Jubilosas
Vuelvan los ríos a batir
                    aguas y palmas
¡Oh! Yania Patria
¡Aleluya!

LA VALLA de metal no es suficiente
Traspasada / llegaría / llegó de repente
La muerte desnuda / sin la ropa
¡Qué noche calurosa!

WITH this discourse I say love
A shared involvement
I say Man

      The voice reaches out across the distance
It grows / it passes through the forests
Rivers clogged with blood

WITH THESE SAME WORDS I SAY GOD
I FIND IT ALL COMPLETE

Through the streets and plazas
Goodness and love
Move across the Lofty Mountains
The rivers begin again to stir
              waters and palm trees
Oh! Yania Patria
Aleluya!

A METAL barricade is not enough
Once death crossed over / it would arrive / it did arrive
Naked death / unclothed
What a hot night!

Nadie estudia su forma ni pregunta
Qué clavo fija ese momento
Dónde se quiebran las preces
Ilumina un fósforo
Tasca el aire en la pequeña área
Junto al bulto de trapos y terecos
Toda Yania marcada y poseída
Por colosos rivales posesivos

Nuevamente sucede lo mismo
Los mártires no son víctimas en balde
Sólo la inevitable ofrece gloria
Sin ropa / sin fatiga / en su gestión continua

YANIA LOPEZ en las Antillas
Eje de calurosas intenciones
En su propia barranca

Con casa de tablones, cartones y yaguas
Hasta que alguien deja caer su tigre
Se hace la oportunidad de defender
La dignidad rodada por el suelo
El viejo cofre con leyes y canciones
      con leyes y oraciones
Queda atrapado debajo de la colcha

No one notices its shape nor asks
Which nail catches that moment
Where prayers are broken
A match lights the darkness
Splitting the air in the cramped space
Next to the bundle of rags and junk
All Yania branded and enslaved
By giant possessive rivals

It happens over and over
The martyrs are not victims in vain
Only the inevitable will bring glory
Naked / relentless / in its unchanging course

YANIA LOPEZ in the Antilles
Center of warmth and good will
On her own cliff

With a house made of planks, cardboard and palm hemp
Until someone lets his tiger pounce
The opportunity is there to defend
Her honor thrown to the floor
The old chest containing laws and songs
       containing laws and prayers
Is left forgotten under the covers

SE SIENTE GANAS DE REIR / DICE EL COJITO AL VER
LAS CABRIOLAS DE QUIENES OBSERVAN LA IMAGEN
PEGADA A LA PARED / AQUELLA DE LA FOTOMATON /
LA DEJARON ASI / SIN POLVO / SIN ROUGE /
DESGREÑADA ENTRE LAS PAREDES QUE EN LA LUNA
NUEVA / LAS TERMITAS CONVIERTEN EN ENCAJES /
LA CASA ES UN HUECO RODEADO DE UNA CAPA
SUCIA DE PINTURA CASCADA

LA deja así / desnuda
      La sábana rasgada
Bajo un cielo sin techo
      Y no sería nada
Y no sería nadie
Sólo polvo
Eso no es obsceno / quién sabe baladí
      Aquel llorar de penas
El tonto suena los nudillos de las manos
Se deja caer sobre un jergón
Cuenta Cinco Siglos / Los Años / Meses /
          Días / Horas / Minutos y
Todas las afrentas con que quieren destruir a
                      Yania López

IT MAKES YOU FEEL LIKE LAUGHING / SAYS THE
CRIPPLE AS HE WATCHES THE SILLY REACTIONS OF
THOSE WHO SEE HER IMAGE PLASTERED ON THE WALL
OF THE PHOTOMAT / THEY LEFT HER LIKE THAT /
WITH NO POWDER / NO ROUGE / DISHEVELED BEHIND
WALLS / TERMITES ARE MAKING INTO LACE / UNDER
THE NEW MOON / THE HOUSE IS A HOVEL ENCASED IN
A DIRTY COAT OF PEELING PAINT

HE abandons her like that / naked
      Her sheet ripped
Under an open sky
      And she would be nothing
And she would be nobody
Only dust
That's not obscene / who would think it trivial
      To cry about pain
The idiot cracks his knuckles
Throws himself down on a pallet
He Counts Five Centuries / The Years / Months /
          Days / Hours / Minutes and
All the crimes committed in an attempt to destroy
                      Yania López

LA irrevocable renuncia de Yania
A las baladas de Bob Dylan
A la voz gutural de Makeba
Al ritmo lascivo de la Donna Summer
El tigre / su exterminio-catástrofe
Imaginan su retrato de muerta
Las pupilas como salones de Museo
                  con su rostro colgado
La caminan hasta el fondo o la derrota
El cortejo con voces de cantantes de la Patria

A
D
I
O
S / Yania / Tierra / Esclava / Jamás

En las Montañas Jubilosas caen las hojas
Doblan elegías
Cierto / El tonto se divierte con el movimiento
                            pendular
De una luz vecina
Alrededor del círculo le atrae la periferia de
                  sombras agazapadas
                  multiplicándose

YANIA'S complete rejection
Of Bob Dylan's ballads
Of Makeba's gutteral voice
Of Donna Summer's sexy rhythm
The tiger / her devastation-ruin
They imagine her death mask
Her pupils like Museum rooms
                      with her face hung
They walk with her to the end or to defeat
The funeral procession with the voices of singers of the Motherland

G
O
O
D
B
Y
E / Yania / Tierra / Slave / Never

In the Lofty Mountains the leaves fall
They compose elegies
It is true / The idiot amuses himself with the swinging
                                      motion
Of a nearby light
His attention is drawn to the circle's edge by
                      shadows crouched
                      multiplying

MUERE de soslayo Yania López
A los asistentes dentro de aquellas paredes
Sin palabras en la casa oscura
Nadie quiere ver el rostro de Yania
Azotado su rostro por la explotación
          Me recago en ellos / Cobardes /
Viva / Así hubiera dicho Yania

Un rudo golpe
              La pisada de un soldado
El golpe prende la soledad
              Un grito lo detiene
Quién bajo el peso baja el picaporte
De la puerta más ancha
Desde el callado silencio de los abecedarios
Otra voz interroga
Quién coloca en cruz las manos de Yania

YANIA López is dying behind those walls
Her back turned to her supporters
Speechless in the dark house
No one wants to see Yania's face
Her face disfigured by exploitation
        I shit on them / Cowards /
Viva! / That's what Yania would have said

A hard blow
              A soldier's bootstep
A blow seizes the silence
              A cry makes him stop
Who dares to unlatch
The widest door
From the hushed silence of school books
Another voice asks
Who will cross Yania's hands

UNOS NIÑOS DELGADOS / HAMBREADOS / HAPAPIENTOS / CORREN POR LA CALLE / GRITAN MALAS PALABRAS / BLASFEMIAS / BROMEAN / TIENEN LIBROS Y CUADERNOS / EL COJITO CONOCE LAS MONTAÑAS JUBILOSAS / CORREN Y GRITAN LAS MAS GRANDES MALAPALABRAS / LAS REPITEN / EN LAS ANTILLAS CARGAN LOS BARCOS DE TESOROS COMO CARGABAN LAS CARABELAS DEL FINIQUITO 400 DEL 500 / 600 / 700 / 800 / 900 ¡JURO QUE NO LLEGAREMOS ASI AL 2000! / GRITAN CON DIGNIDAD HASTA SUS MORADAS / EL COJITO NO SE DA POR VENCIDO / A YANIA LOPEZ LA CAMINAN HASTA EL FINAL DE TODAS LAS DERROTAS / HASTA EL EQUIVOCO FINAL DE TODAS LAS DERROTAS POR POSEERLA SUYA

Yania López vestida
Yania López desnuda
En medio de los cumplimientos reconocen
Su vergüenza y la degradación a que es sometida

SOME SKINNY CHILDREN / HUNGRY / RAGGED / ARE
RUNNING THROUGH THE STREET / SHOUTING DIRTY
WORDS / CURSES / THEY ARE JOKING / THEY HAVE BOOKS
AND NOTEBOOKS / THE CRIPPLE KNOWS THE LOFTY
MOUNTAINS / THEY RUN AND SHOUT THE BIGGEST SWEAR-
WORDS / OVER AND OVER / IN THE ANTILLES THEY ARE
LOADING THE TREASURE BOATS LIKE THEY LOADED THE
CARAVELS AT THE CLOSE OF 400 / 500 / 600 / 700 / 800 / 900 /
I SWEAR THAT WE WON'T GO TO 2000 LIKE THIS! / THEY
SHOUT WITH PRIDE ALL THE WAY HOME / THE CRIPPLE
REFUSES TO GIVE UP / THEY WALK WITH YANIA LOPEZ
TO HER FINAL DEFEAT / TO WHAT THEY THOUGHT
WAS HER FINAL DEFEAT TO MAKE HER THEIR OWN

Yania López clothed
Yania López naked
In the middle of paying their respects they recognize
Her shame the humiliation to which she is subjected

YANIA despierta / Yania dormida /
La caminan / Reconocen el golpe de las botas
Respiran con la expresión fija
Lívida
Vidriosa
Observan en alta mar las redes con que pescan
						Islas

Cansados cambian el peso de la carga

Nunca indiferentes al hecho
No entienden / Muchos no quieren entenderlo
Sueltan carcajadas / Caen risas
La caminan sin llegar hasta el fondo
Yania oro / Yania plata / Yania bauxita
Yania cacao / Yania azúcar / Yania café

YANIA awake / Yania asleep /
They walk with her / They recognize the pounding of boots
They breathe with their expression fixed
Livid
Glassy
On the high seas they can see the nets used to fish for
$$\text{Islands}$$

Exhausted they shift the weight of the load

Never bored with their task
They don't understand / Many don't want to understand it
They split their guts / Burst out laughing
They walk with her but never reach the end
Yania gold / Yania silver / Yania bauxite
Yania cacao / Yania sugar / Yania coffee

SIEMPRE inmersa en las épocas del fuego
En la noche recostada a la noche
Pobre lloro / Pobre grito consciente
La guerra no es un poema
Llena los huecos de esqueletos

En un pasadizo de cuchillos y tijeras
Yania sangra oro
Devuelve el azúcar
Sabe que la Historia comienza en Marién
Con un Fortín de tablas de navío / que
Antes / muy cortésmente / la Paz vivía junto a
                                        gaviotas
                                        palomas y
                                        maizales

Ahora la Paz observa cascos y lanzas
Para el presente y futuras escenas
Ve romper el idilio permanente
La sorprende el violento nacimiento

La historia nace en Marién
Con la palabra manifiesto del gran Almirante

ALWAYS engulfed in the ages of fire
At night she reclines into the night
A pitiful sob / A pitiful waking cry
War is not a poem
It covers the ground with skeletons

In an alleyway of knives and scissors
Yania bleeds gold
Vomits sugar
She knows that History begins in Marién
With a Fort built from ship planks / that
Before / very respectfully / Peace lived in harmony with
                                                          seagulls
                                                        doves and
                                                        cornfields

Now Peace sees helmets and lances
Dominate present and future scenes
She sees the timeless idyll broken
The violent birth surprises her

History is born in Marién
With the imperial command of the great Admiral

EN Marién se inicia la Conquista
Al nativo le sorprende el forastero
Que construye derrotas
Rompe a intervalos
El corazón de sus dioses de madera / o barro
Se apodera del oro
De otros bienes y riquezas

Yania sabe que la Paz
No transita por caminos de odio
Y usted / blanco / indio / negro / mestizo o mulato
Usted sabe / Desde entonces la Paz se muere de
                                          vergüenza
                                          por usted
                                          Señor Usted

IN Marién the Conquest begins
The native is surprised by the foreigner
Who constructs destruction
Breaks from time to time
The hearts of his gods of wood / or clay
He steals the gold
Other goods and riches

Yania knows that Peace
Doesn't travel on paths of hatred
And that you / white / indian / black / mestizo or mulatto
You know / Since that time Peace has been dying of
                                            shame
                                            because of you
                                            Sir you

EL COJITO MAS COJO O MENOS COJO CONTINUA POR DONDE CAMINAN A YANIA / DOBLA CON EL CORTEJO OTRA ESQUINA / ESCUCHA MUSICA Y PARTE DEL NOTICIARIO NACIONAL EN UN RADIO ANUNCIO COCA COLA / GIRA EL GLOBO DE UNA TIERRA TRISTE QUE ILUMINA EL MISMO SOL DE CARLOS V / CAMINAN HACIA ATRAS LA LIBERTAD Y LA JUSTICIA / LOS PERROS LADRAN SEPARADOS POR UNA SOLIDA PARED / SE MUEVEN SIN RUMBO / NADIE PUEDE RESTARLE NADA A YANIA / DICE EL COJITO / EN LA PARED HAY UNA GRIETA Y UN SLOGAN / LAS SOMBRAS SE SUCEDEN / SUDA / SE CANSA / TARROS DE AMAPOLAS Y OTRAS FLORES LLORONAS DUERMEN MARCHITAS EN EL SALON DEL QUE MANDA / SI / COJO SIEMPRE / EL COJITO CONTINUA A SU LADO / NI LUZ / NI AGUA / NI PERIODICO / NI RADIO / NI TELEVISION DECENTES / NADA SERIO / NI EL NOTARIO NI EL JUEZ / NI LA VERGUENZA / CUANDO DANTE ESCRIBE LA DIVINA COMEDIA HA CAMINADO LA MITAD DE SU VIDA / CADA AMANECER CON LAS PRIMERAS LUCES / EL TEMOR SE ENSANCHA / EL COJITO BUSCA UNA ESCALERA PARA SUBIR A LA LIBERTAD / TODAS ESAS BANCARROTAS NO CABEN EN ARCHIVOS / LA GAVETA DE INFORMES COLONIALES CRUJE CUANDO SE HABLA DE SOBERANIA TOTAL

THE CRIPPLE LIMPING CONTINUES ALONGSIDE AS THEY WALK WITH YANIA / HE TURNS ANOTHER CORNER WITH THE FUNERAL PROCESSION / HE HEARS MUSIC AND PART OF THE NATIONAL NEWS ON A COCA-COLA SPONSORED RADIO SPOT / THE GLOBE SPINS ON A SAD LAND LIT BY THE SAME SUN THAT SHONE UPON CARLOS V / FREEDOM AND JUSTICE ARE LOSING GROUND / THE BARKING DOGS ARE HELD AT BAY BY A SOLID WALL / THEY MOVE AIMLESSLY / NO ONE CAN TAKE ANYTHING AWAY FROM YANIA / SAYS THE CRIPPLE / THERE IS A CRACK IN THE WALL AND A SLOGAN / THE SHADOWS MOVE ALONG IN SUCCESSION / HE SWEATS / HE TIRES / JARS OF POPPIES AND OTHER WEEPING FLOWERS LIE WILTING IN THE MASTER'S SALON / YES / LIMPING STILL / THE CRIPPLE CONTINUES ALONG AT HER SIDE / NO DECENT LIGHT / NO WATER / NO NEWSPAPER / NO RADIO / NO TELEVISION / NOTHING SERIOUS / NO LAWYER NOR JUDGE / NO SHAME / WHEN DANTE WRITES THE DIVINE COMEDY HALF HIS LIFE HAS PASSED / WITH THE FIRST LIGHT OF EACH NEW DAY / FEAR INCREASES / THE CRIPPLE LOOKS FOR A STAIR-WAY TO CLIMB TO FREEDOM / ALL THE BANKRUPT-CIES WON'T FIT IN THE FILES / THE COLONIAL BU-REAU OF INFORMATION MOANS WHEN ANYONE SPEAKS ABOUT TOTAL SOVEREIGNTY

EN las Montañas Jubilosas
Quedan quienes aprecian cabalmente
                         con dolor
De las Montañas salen lágrimas
Yania dolor de amor herido / mártir
Ella misma su Tierra
Desposeída por absurdos argonautas

IN the Lofty Mountains
There are still some who remember
                              painfully
Tears stream down from the Mountains
Yania the pain of wounded love / martyr
She herself her Land
Dispossessed by crazed argonauts

SOLO LOS ARBOLES CON SUS BARBAS PERENNES
VERDEAZULES / SOLO EL RIO RETORNA A SU
FUENTE Y DA PAZ / SOLO YANIA A VECES CUENTA
CON EL CANTO DE AMOR / DE HEROISMO Y DE
SABIDURIA DE LAS MUJERES / COMO ISLAS EN
EL CONTEXTO DE SU ISLA / SIN SABER EL LUGAR
DE SU DESTINO

Sólo ríen las Montañas para Yania
Ella misma Montaña / Ella misma dolor
Ella — tal vez un día — sonrisa
Ella su Tierra
Desposeída por absurdos argonautas
Sólo ella sollozo
Sólo ella
        consume
                tristeza

ONLY THE TREES WITH THEIR PERENNIAL BLUE-GREEN BEARDS / ONLY THE RIVER RETURNS TO ITS SOURCE AND BRINGS PEACE / ONLY YANIA AT TIMES RELIES ON THE SONG OF LOVE / OF THE COURAGE AND WISDOM OF WOMEN / LIKE ISLANDS SURROUNDING HER ISLAND / NOT KNOWING WHERE DESTINY WILL TAKE HER

Only the Mountains laugh for Yania
She herself Mountain / She herself pain
She — perhaps someday — a smile
She her Land
Dispossessed by crazed argonauts
Only she a sob
Only she
       consumes
              sadness

YANIA vomita oro
                sangre
                        azúcar
Sabe que la historia comienza en Marién
Con un cacique / luego dos / después todos /
Que los Encomenderos / Los Repartimientos
Los indios / los negros
Base de la Tragedia Humana / Llamada Civilización
Desde un día 25 todas las golondrinas
Durante cinco siglos
Continuamente trazan círculos
Sobre los mástiles de los navíos
Con cargazones de lanceros en busca de tesoros
Con toneles de vino para alentar la abulia

Bloques de piedras del Alcázar
Torre del Homenaje / La Catedral y
                        otros monumentos
Donde albergan / claro / depredadores de
Aragón y Castilla
En resumen / de toda la Ibérica Península

YANIA vomits gold
                blood
                        sugar
She knows that history begins in Marién
With one cacique / then two / finally all of them /
That the Encomenderos / the Repartimientos
The indians / the blacks
The foundation of the Human Tragedy / Called Civilization
Since day 25 all the swallows
For five centuries
Continually trace circles
Above the ships' masts
Carrying huge cargos of soldiers in search of treasures
With kegs of wine to ward off boredom

Blocks of stone from Alcázar
Tower of Homage / The Cathedral and
                              other monuments
Where they / naturally / shelter pillagers from
Aragón and Castilla
In fact / from the whole Iberian Peninsula

YANIA con aire sugestivo
Con profundo amor por su tierra / carne-hueso
Aún en posición incómoda
                         Lamenta la aventura
La caída en manos de colonos
                         Desde aquella mañana
Diciembre 25 / Año 92 del 400
Las chispas con cenizas
Los hijos rayadores de yuca
De la guáyiga
                 Lavadores del oro de los ríos
                 El quinto para el Rey
                 El resto para depredadores

En espejos sucesivos
Las edades del tiempo
Reflejan ríos / oro y extraños personajes

YANIA with a seductive air
With deep love for her land / her flesh and blood
Still in a difficult position
                        She mourns the adventure
Falling into the hands of the colonizers
                        From that morning
December 25 / Year 92 of 400
Ashes with sparks
Her children, shredders of yucca
Of guáyiga
                        Washers of the gold from the rivers
                        One fifth for the King
                        The rest for the pillagers

In successive mirrors
Through the ages of time
The rivers reflect / gold and strange characters

EL COJITO CONOCE LAS HISTORIAS DE ANTES Y DESPUES / REMEMORA LAS COSAS APRENDIDAS / LLENO DE TRISTES PENSAMIENTOS SIGUE GUARDANDO EN EL ARCA DE SU MEMORIA EL DESOLADO PAISAJE / SUS DEVASTACIONES / LO QUE ENSEÑA EL ENRIQUILLO DE GALVAN / LA OBRA MEMORABLE DE UN AUTOR QUE SIGUE AL INVASOR.

THE CRIPPLE KNOWS THE STORIES FROM BEFORE
AND AFTER / HE REMEMBERS THE THINGS HE HAS
LEARNED / FULL OF SAD THOUGHTS HE KEEPS THE
DESOLATE COUNTRYSIDE STORED IN HIS MEMORY /
ITS DEVASTATIONS / THE THINGS THAT ENRIQUILLO
DE GALVÁN TEACHES / THE CLASSIC WORK OF AN
AUTHOR WHO CHRONICLES THE INVADER.

LA TIERRA rota / Desbrozada / la
Abre clara la pezuña del equino
El canto de la Reina
Señora de la Isla
Empezado con la vida
El Areíto obsequio de la
      Dama doña Anacaona
Danzan / Saludan sus Vírgenes
      desnudas / saludan

Ovando ordena el exterminio

Cae la Reina
Los caciques
Las vírgenes
La gente de Jaragua
    c
   a
    e

THE LAND destroyed / Leveled / split
Open by the horse's hoof
The song of the Queen
Mistress of the Island
Born with her life
The Areito a gift for the
                      Lady doña Anacaona
They dance / Her virgins beckon
                    naked / they beckon

Ovando orders their extermination

The Queen falls
The caciques
The virgins
The people of Jaragua
              f
            a
             l
              l

EN su incómoda posición
Ella Isla por la mitad un día
Planos cambiantes en todos los espejos
Como paquetes de láminas en una vieja moto
Para cargar películas
Desde la mañana 25
Diciembre 92 del 400
Cuando hidalgos / hijodalgos e hideputas
Traían posters con retratos de reyes y de reinas
Y de esclavas cargadas de abalorios

Justo lo que sobra / lamentablemente
Para que Yania vomitara verde
Todo lo que se carga en naves que regresan
Para que Yania vomitara verde / verde
Su muerte verde a largo plazo / verde

IN her difficult position
She an Island one day divided down the middle
Boundaries changing in all the mirrors
Like the frames in an old
Movie projector
Since the morning of the 25th
December 92 of 400
When hidalgos / sons-of-somebody and sons-of-bitches
Brought banners with pictures of kings and queens
And of female slaves adorned with glass beads

Just enough / sadly
For Yania to vomit green
Everything loaded on ships to send back
So that Yania would vomit green / green
Her green death for the long haul / green

YANIA presente en los Areítos
Yania muerta en los Areítos
Yania rediviva / siempre viva
No se oculta al aviso del fotuto
Al tintineo de pequeñas olivas
A la melodía de ocarinas y silbatos

Danza su pueblo / Danza
Inesperado exterminio lo sacude
Muere su pueblo
Sobre su vientre escucha
El recién llegado equino

YANIA alive in the Areítos
Yania dead in the Areítos
Yania reborn / everliving
Never deaf to the bugle call
To the tinkling of bells
To the melody of whistles and flutes

Her people dance / Dance
Shattered by the unforeseen annihilation
Her people die
On her belly she hears
The newly arrived horse

EL COJITO / DEBE HABER ALGUIEN QUE ESTE BIEN
INFORMADO / ALGUIEN AQUI QUE REDACTE
INFORMES DE TODOS LOS NEGOCIOS DE COLONIAS /
ALGUIEN QUE JURE QUE UN INVASOR HA HECHO
COSA HONESTA.

Yania reconoce al pie de cinco siglos
La Corte ambiciosa de Virreyes
Los Garay / Ovando / Tostado / Dávila /
    Caballero y otros tantos
Cuyo intenso sabor mercurial
Montesino condena

THE CRIPPLE / THERE MUST BE SOMEONE WHO
IS WELL-INFORMED / SOMEONE HERE WHO RECORDS
ALL COLONIAL BUSINESS / SOMEONE WHO MAY
SWEAR THAT AN INVADER HAS DONE SOMETHING
HONEST.

At the end of five centuries Yania recognizes
The ambitious Court of Viceroys
The Garays / Ovandos / Tostados / Dávilas /
      Caballeros and so many others
Whose intense volatile character
Montesino condemns

ARDE LA TIERRA La Colonia

        Llegan de África
        Las naves de España
        Portugal
        Holanda
        Inglaterra
        Llegan de África las naves

EN la Plaza Mayor
Subastan a los esclavos negros
Los negociadores de vidas

¡Puñetero negocio!
Venden al abuelo y al padre de
Teodora y Micaela Ginés
Esclavas / luego libertas en
Santiago de los Caballeros
Antes de 1580 residentes en Cuba
Las dos primeras damas músicas
            en aquel territorio

THE LAND BURNS The Colony

        They come from Africa
        Ships from Spain
        Portugal
        Holland
        England
        Ships come from Africa

IN the Main Plaza
The merchants of lives
Auction off black slaves

Filthy business!
They sell the grandfather and father of
Teodora and Micaela Ginés
Female slaves / later freed in
Santiago de los Caballeros
Residents of Cuba before 1580
The first two lady musicians
                in that territory

MICAELA en La Habana
TEODORA en Oriente
Tocadoras de vihuela y de bandola

"—Dónde está la Ma' Teodora?
—Rajando la leña está.
—Con su palo y su bandola
—Rajando la leña está.
—Dónde está que no la veo?
—Rajando la leña está.
—Rajando la leña está.
—Rajando la leña está
—Rajando la leña está.
—Rajando la leña está".

MICAELA in Havana
TEODORA in Oriente
Players of the bandola and the vihuela

"—Where is Ma' Teodora?
—She's cutting firewood.
—With her bow and her bandola
—She's cutting firewood.
—Where is she? I don't see her.
—She's cutting firewood.
—She's cutting firewood.
—She's cutting firewood.
—She's cutting firewood.
—She's cutting firewood."

ARDE la tierra / La Colonia
Quién toca el laúd en el Alcázar
Oh Mencía triste rosa mestiza
El arpa y el laúd y tu amorosa espera
La Virreina y Las Casas
Celebran tu unión con Enriquillo

QUE damas llegan al Convento
La Madre Priora doña Leonor de Ovando
Hace versos / canta dama Leonor
Despierta / Yania dice sus versos
La letra de los cantos de
Elvira de Mendoza
           se pierden
Cinco siglos de lluvias y de lunas
De odio / de saqueo / de vientos y de soles
                              sin Elvira

THE LAND burns / The Colony
Who is playing the lute in Alcázar
Oh Mencía sad mestiza rose
The harp and the lute and your amorous waiting
The Vicereine and Las Casas
Celebrate your union with Enriquillo

LOOK at the ladies arriving at the Convent
The Mother Prioress doña Leonor de Ovando
Composes verses / lady Leonor sings
She wakes up / Yania sings her verses
The lyrics of the songs of
Elvira de Mendoza
                 are lost
Five centuries of rains and moons
Of hatred / of looting / of winds and suns
                             without Elvira

En el 63 del 1500
Hawkins sale de Inglaterra
Con corsarios, piratas, bucaneros
                      y otros elementos fatales

Llega desde Sierra Leona a Puerto Plata
En la Vieja Isabela impone el cambalache
                      de cueros
                      de azúcar
Por la triste mercancía de los esclavos
                      negros
Humilla al Monopolio del Imperio Español

86 del 1500
Desde Londres Isabel la reina virgen
Mujer que lee a Maquiavelo
Usa a sus súbditos piratas
Saquean los tesoros del mundo
Aquí Sir Francis Drake
Despoja / daña la Ciudad Colonial
Condiciona su marcha
                a cambio
                de millonaria suma

In the year 63 of 1500
Hawkins leaves England
With plunderers, pirates, buccaneers
                      and other murderous types

He comes from Sierra Leon to Puerto Plata
In Old Isabela he directs the exchange
                      of hides
                      of sugar
For the miserable merchandise of black
                      slaves
He humiliates the Monopoly of the Spanish Empire

The year 86 of 1500
From London Elizabeth the Virgin Queen
A woman who reads Machiavelli
Uses her pirate subjects
To loot the treasures of the world
Here Sir Francis Drake
Rapes / destroys the Colonial City
Redirects its history
                      in exchange
                      for a millionaire's sum

YANIA observa
Se levantan ingenios / se penetra su vientre
Se lava oro
Para los reinos de Europa Occidental
El negro explotado como bestia
Los extraños / padres / padrastros del saqueo
Yania como una rosa verde o una rosa de fuego
Las Montañas baten agua
truenos
      relámpagos
           rayos y
                  centellas
El hambre llena el transcurso del tiempo

EL COJITO SUBE / BAJA / SE PIERDE / ES UN JODERSE SIEMPRE / ELLA LO SABE / EL COJITO FLAQUEA / CASI CAE / NO CAE / SE LEVANTA / SE ENDEREZA / SUELE VOCIFERAR / MIRARSE AL ESPEJO Y PREGUNTARSE A SU CARA / POR QUE JODERSE SIEMPRE

YANIA watches
Sugar mills are erected / her womb is penetrated
Gold is washed
For the kingdoms of Western Europe
The black man exploited like a beast
The foreigners / fathers / step-fathers of the looting
Yania like a green rose or a flaming rose
The mountains stir up water
thunder
        lightening
                thunderbolts and
                        flashes
Hunger fills the course of time

THE CRIPPLE PACES BACK / AND FORTH / HE IS LOST / WE ALWAYS GET FUCKED OVER / SHE KNOWS IT / THE CRIPPLE FALTERS / HE ALMOST FALLS / HE DOESN'T FALL / HE GETS UP / HE STRAIGHTENS UP / HE SCREAMS / LOOK AT YOURSELF IN THE MIRROR AND ASK YOURSELF / WHY DO WE ALWAYS GET FUCKED OVER

EN aquel Diciembre 25
Año 92 del 400
Comienza la Historia de la Madre Nuestra
La Tierra es Yania López
A los nativos llega la muerte despiadada
Entra en las casas
Con la historia se inicia la fatal opresión
El suelo gris de muchas capas
El hambre en los villorios
Pueblos y ciudades / Simetría de miseria
Desechos de desechos
Hasta Napoleón pretende tomar la Isla entera
(Sin Edith Piaf la noche es tenebrosa)

Oh tristes años de la España Boba
Vuelven las rondas y las nanas vuelven
La mismas lanzas las traspasan

ON that December 25
Year 92 of 400
The History of Our Mother begins
The Land is Yania López
A heartless death comes to the natives
It enters the houses
With history begins the fatal oppression
Layer upon layer of gray dirt
Hunger in the slums
Towns and cities / Symmetry of misery
Dregs of the dregs
Even Napoleon tries to take the whole Island
(Without Edith Piaf the night is ominous)

Oh the painful years of España Boba
The nursery rhymes are back the nannies are back
The same lances run through them

Yania sabe que son damas
La Casa del Cordón las ve llegar
Entregan sus joyas / su dinero
Yania sabe que son damas
Damas rescatan la ciudad

En el 88 el Monopolio Mercantil Hispano
Hispano naufraga con la Invencible
Armada
        Osorio se aprovecha / destruye
        las ciudades / los pueblos de la
        costa norte
        por delante el ganado
        detrás los pobladores
        muerte / desolación
        Osorio amo / dueño / señor
        de nuevos pueblos y villas

        En el 5 del 600 los veleros cambian
                las rutas
                sobre la mar océana
                se acentúan la
                ruina / la
                muerte
                la despoblación
                en La Española

Yania knows they are ladies
The Treasury authorities see them arrive
They hand over their jewelry / their money
Yania knows they are ladies
Ladies will rescue the city

In the year 88 the Hispanic Mercantile Monopoly
Hispanic shipwrecks with the Invincible
Armada
        Osorio seizes the moment / destroys
        cities / towns of the
        north coast
        first the livestock
        then the townspeople
        death / desolation
        Osorio master / owner / lord
        of new towns and villas

        In the year 5 of 600 the ships change
                their routes
                over the oceans
                bringing more
                destruction
                death
                depopulation
                to Hispaniola

AÑOS de Boyer / Herard / Borgellá y Carrié
Desechos de desechos
Horizonte negado a la esperanza
Tam-tam tambores de Occidente

Sube el llanto de Dominga de los
Núñez de Cáceres
De Francisca Hurtado / inmolada
La misma suerte imponen a Gregoria
                                      Ceferina y
                                      Felipa las hijas de
                                      Medina

YEARS of Boyer / Herard / Borgellá and Carrié
Scum of the scum
A horizon without hope
The tam-tam of drums from the West

The screams rise from Dominga de los
Núñez de Cáceres
From Francisca Hurtado / slaughtered
They order the same fate for Gregoria
                                          Ceferina and
                                          Felipa daughters of
                                          Medina

EN Galindo
      Agueda
      Anita y
      Marcelina Andújar
      Vírgenes profanadas
      Violadas por la insania
      Asesinadas
      Oh / repudio total

Las tropas avanzan por todos los cuadrantes
En la tierra de Yania / desnudas y rotas
                          están las contrapuertas
Nadie quiere la noche / El salto a las tinieblas
En todas las proximidades se repara en
                          terribles bochornos
En el centro de la tormenta se respira a secas
Prevalecen las noches desveladas

IN Galindo
>   Agueda
>   Anita and
>   Marcelina Andújar
>   Dishonored virgins
>   Raped by madness
>   Murdered
>   Oh / total damnation

The troops advance from every quadrant
Of Yania's land / broken and bare
                        are the outer doors
Nobody wants the night to come / The leap into darkness
In all the surrounding areas they are overcome by
                        terrible suffocating heat
In the eye of the storm they gasp for breath
Sleepless nights prevail

EL COJITO TIRA SU SOMBRERO AL AIRE / VALIOSAS TODAS LAS COMPAÑERAS / LA HISTORIA RECONOCE A JUANA DE ARCO / JUANA SE LEVANTA PARA LIBERAR A SU PUEBLO / JUANA ACUSADA DE LA GUERRA Y EL FUEGO / JUANA RESPONDE / YO SOY LA CULPABLE / EL CORTEJO DE YANIA OBSERVA EN EL MAR LOS NAVIOS Y LAS REDES CON QUE PESCAN ISLAS / TERRITORIOS Y HOMBRES / UNA FAMILIA DESDE UNA COLINA ODIA UN CAMINAR QUE NUNCA SE TERMINA / CAMINAN A YANIA / YANIA REDIVIVA / DICE ROSA EN EL EXILIO / YO ENTREGUE LA BANDERA / MARIA TRINIDAD EN EL PATIBULO / YO LLEVE LA POLVORA / EN LA PRISION JUNTO A SOCORRO SANCHEZ / GRITA BALBINA PEÑA / YO CUIDO SU HONRA.

THE CRIPPLE TOSSES HIS HAT IN THE AIR / ALL THE COMPAÑERAS ARE BRAVE / HISTORY RECOGNIZES JOAN OF ARC / JOAN RISES TO FREE HER PEOPLE / JOAN ACCUSED OF WAR AND FIRE / JOAN RESPONDS / I AM THE GUILTY ONE / YANIA'S FUNERAL PROCESSION WATCHES THE SEA THE SHIPS AND THE NETS THEY USE TO FISH FOR ISLANDS / TERRITORIES AND MEN / A FAMILY FROM THE HILLSIDE HATES AN ENDLESS PROCESSION / THEY WALK WITH YANIA / YANIA REVIVES / ROSA SAYS FROM EXILE / I DELIVERED THE FLAG / MARIA TRINIDAD FROM THE GALLOWS / I TOOK THE GUN-POWDER / IN THE PRISON NEXT TO SOCORRO SANCHEZ / BALBINA PEÑA SHOUTS / I'LL DEFEND YOUR HONOR.

EN la misma puerta del desafío trágico
Los activistas de La Filantrópica
     Difraz de cultura
     Proclamas y gestos
     En la escena mujeres
     Ligadas a los héroes
     Empresarios y autores

Las mujeres demandan sacrificio / Convencidas
Sin guerrear en las batallas / Sin huellas de sollozos

Con futuro triunfal
    María Luisa del Rosario
    María Guadalupe
    María del Amparo
    María de los Dolores
Transmiten a los espectadores el fervor inminente
        para ganar la tierra
        soñada libre

AT the very door of the tragic struggle
The activists from The Philanthropic Foundation
                              Under the guise of culture
                              Proclamations and gestures
                              On the stage women
                              Loyal to the heroes
                              Leaders and authors

The women demand sacrifice / Convinced
Without fighting in combat / Without a trace of tears

With a triumphant future
                María Luisa del Rosario
                María Guadalupe
                María del Amparo
                María de los Dolores
Inspire in the spectators an overwhelming passion
                                    to win back the land
                                    they have dreamed free

Sin duda alguna se amplía el poder expresivo
La secundan / Con trazos de aplomados parlamentos
Con el ritual del símbolo perenne
Mariana Rafaela de la Concha
María Paula y Agueda Bona
Las Alfau Bustamante
Abrazadas penetran / llenan su papel

    María Antonia de la Concha
    María de Jesús Pina
    Todas con voces de desesperado rumbo
    como apóstoles hablan
    Sin reposo y sosiego
    Entre pánico y sombras
    Rechazan con obras de Teatro
    Se exponen por su Patria al martirio

Con concepto de base / En busca de un escudo / Sin pólvora
Por sobre tierras suyas golpeadas / Se levantan
Cubren el espacio con su voz / Con sus cuerpos
Hecatombe y vorágine / La voz de esas mujeres

Without any doubt their power of expression is growing
They exercise it / With the style of self-assured parliaments
With the ritual of the perennial symbol
Mariana Rafaela de la Concha
María Paula and Agueda Bona
The Alfau Bustamante sisters
They enter the stage arm-in-arm / They play their role

>	María Antonia de la Concha
>	María de Jesús Pina
>	All with voices of desperation
>	like apostles they speak
>	Without rest or relaxation
>	Between panic and shadows
>	They protest with Theatre
>	They offer themselves to martyrdom for their Homeland

With a common goal / Looking for a rallying banner / Without gunpowder
Over their battered lands / They rise up
Spread their voice across the land / With their bodies
Hecatomb and vortex / The voice of those women

Toda la piel de los espectadores / quema
Se clama ser libre
La tan amada Tierra
De una Isla por la mitad un día
Aún a la intemperie extranjeras banderas
                                                   en los topes
Cuándo la insignia propia

        En el escenario se denuncian los crímenes
        Se exaltan ideales nobles
        Con las obras
        LA VIUDA DE PADILLA / que enciende la
        protesta
        Y reclama derechos

Sin vacilaciones cruzan el escenario
Las valientes / En el cartel se anuncian

    ROMA LIBRE
    EL DIA 23 EN CADIZ
    LA FUENTE DE LA JUDIA
    LOS TEMPLARIOS
    EL CALIFA DE BAGDAD

The flesh of all the spectators / burns
The Land so beloved
Cries out to be free
An Island divided down the middle one day
Outside there are still foreign flags
                                     on the flagpoles
When will it be our own flag

    On the stage crimes are denounced
    Noble ideals are praised
    With these plays
    THE WIDOW PADILLA / which incites the
    protest
    Demands rights

Without hesitation they cross the stage
Brave women / The marquee announces

    ROME FREED
    THE 23RD DAY IN CADIZ
    THE FOUNTAIN OF THE JEWESS
    THE KNIGHTS TEMPLAR
    THE CALIPH OF BAGHDAD

Y comedias y dramas de Bobea / Alejandro Pina / y
otros
Todos esperan la respuesta
A las intérpretes llamadas
En su sitio / sin giros / La Española
Abatida por las aguas bravas

And comedies and dramas of Bobea / Alejandro Pina / and others
All await the response
To the actresses
Standing in their place / facing forward / Hispaniola
Battered by the storm-wracked waters

EL PASO crece / El pie avanza
Donde la honra está a la puerta
Donde impecables las viñas brotan zumos
Donde el pasto arde en su fuego

Las tormentas se desatan conmovidas
Nada disimulada la casa de los Duarte
Manuela Diez cultiva Jazmín de Malabar
Lo trajo Filomena / Lo cuida Rosa
Se expresan de conocidos personajes
                        parte de la epopeya
                        para reconquistar la tierra

Hablar Mujeres / Hablar / Mujeres / Hablar
Hurtan a Yania
Acusan a Yania
Desatan la trama como en las novelas

Alientan reconocer las fuerzas
Algo como luchar / No seguir esperando
Las Duarte bajo su techo
Hermoso marco donde la constancia

THE PACE quickens / Footsteps advance
Where honor is at the door
Where the impeccable vineyards burst with juice
Where the meadow burns in its fire

The storms break loose
Nothing conceals The Duarte house
Manuela Diez cultivates Malabar Jasmine
Filomena brought it / Rosa tends it
They speak about well-known personages
                                   part of the epic poem
                                   to reconquer the land

Speak Out Women / Speak Out / Women / Speak Out
They are looting Yania
They are condemning Yania
They unravel the plot as in a novel

They are excited to realize their power
Somewhat like fighting / Not to go on waiting
The Duarte women under their roof
Beautiful structure where perseverance

Ve florecer Jazmín de Malabar
Insignia de la lucha Trinitaria
Se ve en el duelo / en el exilio / en el triunfo
$$\text{o la desgracia}$$
La flor que entrega Manuela a coro
con Rosa Trinitaria
"A esos jóvenes que tienen la recia voluntad
        La firme decisión de triunfar".
La flor / también cuidada por
Francisca
Filomena y
Sandalia / las hijas / las hermanas
La flor que ama María Antonia Bobadilla
        de Juan Pablo primer amor frustrado
La flor que conserva La Nona Prudencia
                      Lluberes
La tan amada del Patricio
También la cuida
María Villeta la compañera del hermano
                      Vicente Celestino

Yania con pose de Venus surrealista
Besa los labios de recodos de ríos y estanques
No abandona su fuerza
            al caótico golpe de Occidente

Sees the Malabar Jasmine flourish
Emblem of the Trinitarian struggle
You can see it in battle / in exile / in triumph
                                         or misfortune
The flower that Manuela delivers in unison
with Rosa Trinitaria
"To those young people who have the strength of will
         The unshakable determination to triumph."
The flower / tended also by
Francisca
Filomena and
Sandalia / daughters / sisters
The flower that María Antonia Bobadilla loves
         She was the first unrequited love of Juan Pablo
The flower kept by Nona Prudencia
                       Lluberes
So loved by the Patriot
María Villeta also tends it
She's the compañera of brother
                       Vicente Celestino

Yania with the pose of a surrealistic Venus
Kisses the lips of riverbends and ponds
Her strength does not fail her
                 under the chaotic blow from the West

El brillo perlado Malabar
Permanece con ella

Son las Duarte tan intensas
Y cargadas de sorpresas
Siempre en la lucha del fuego
      hacen balas y
      vendajes

En su casa o en otra
En el exilio o no
Las Duarte / dice Yania
Nadie tome su sitio
     tan alto
       como el Sol

The bright pearlescent Malabar
Remains with her

The Duarte sisters are so intense
And filled with surprises
Always in the line of fire
           they make bullets and
           bandages

Whether in their house or another
Whether in exile or not
The Duarte women / says Yania
May no one take their place
               as high
                     as the Sun

Las paredes se corren
Vivo Francisco diez veces vivo o muerto
Milochocientoscuarentaicuatrovivo
Vivo por los muertos que fueron y serán

En la cita de honor
Junto al Baluarte
Balbina Peña su mujer
Sigue a Francisco por sus hechos
Sigue a Francisco
         a
        la
        inmortalidad

Cae Andrés Sánchez por la Patria
Cual Polixena de Troya se niega a delatar
Cae María Trinidad Sánchez con su verdad
Cae Francisco del Rosario Sánchez el héroe Trinitario

    Balbina tras las rejas
    Acompaña a Socorro en la prisión

    Son las sombras / Los signos
    Olaya en el jardín de las catástrofes
    Olaya en la bandera

The sets are moved back
Alive Francisco ten times alive or dead
Eighteenfortyfouralive
Alive for the dead who were and will be

At the appointed hour of honor
Next to the Stockade
His wife Balbina Peña
Follows Francisco for her deeds
Follows Francisco
          to
              immortality

Andrés Sánchez falls for his Homeland
And Polixena de Troya refuses to denounce him
María Trinidad Sánchez falls with her secret
The Trinitarian hero Francisco del Rosario Sánchez falls

      Balbina behind bars
      She keeps Socorro company in prison

      These are the shadows / The signs
      Olaya in the garden of disasters
      Olaya in the flag

QUIENES cortan de la rama la flor
                                      tan apreciada
Las mujeres
Quiénes colocan en el pecho de los libertadores
                                      Jazmín de Malabar
Las mujeres
Quiénes de rodillas imploran cuando el
                                      plomo destruye
Las mujeres

Quiénes desconsoladas esperan el
                    cambio de las arremetidas
Las mujeres

Quiénes buscan Palomas de la Paz en
                           un cielo sin techo
Las mujeres

Quiénes ofrecen el amor de mujer a
                           los héroes
Las mujeres

WHO cuts from the branch the most
                              treasured flower
The women
Who places on the breast of the liberators
                              Malabar Jasmine
The women
Who falls to their knees and begs when
                              lead shatters
The women

Who inconsolable awaits the
        exchange of gunfire
The women

Who looks for Doves of Peace in
                              an open sky
The women

Who offers a woman's love to
                              the heroes
The women

Amor carnal de Manuela
Que engendra la casta de los Duarte
Amor carnal de Olaya
Que engendra la casta de los Sánchez
Amor carnal de Ana Josefa Brea
Que engendra la casta de los Mella
Ni Manuela ni Olaya / ni Ana Josefa / han recibido
    cantos
Manuela / Olaya / Ana Josefa / Yania ofrece su
    canto por los héroes nacidos de sus vientres

Oh luz de amplio amor
Amor con todas las fatigas
Amor por tantos hombres

Amor de luz en las calamidades
Oh Yania / Oh tierra de las gestas
    Están los compañeros
    Derrotan las ofensas

Manuela's carnal love
That begets the Duarte lineage
Olaya's carnal love
That begets the Sánchez lineage
Ana Josefa Brea's carnal love
That begets the Mella lineage
Not for Manuela nor Olaya / nor for Ana Josefa / has any
    song been sung
Manuela / Olaya / Ana Josefa / Yania offers her
    song for the heroes born of your wombs

Oh light of complete love
Love with all the hardships
Love for so many men

Love shines light on the disasters
Oh Yania / Oh land of heroic deeds
    The compañeros are here
    They are fending off the attacks

ANA JOSEFA BREA
        la de Matías Ramón Mella
Incansable colaboradora en la empresa
        por la liberación
En Cuba queda un vástigo / De su línea nace
Lucha y muere contra la tiranía

En Moca en su casa de palma
        humilde hermosa casa
Contadora de gestas
Vive Matilde Mella / Ciega
Casi al cumplir un siglo
Sufre calamidades
La rodea el respeto del pueblo
Es la nieta de Mella
Motor de la contienda
Grande en el trabucazo
        del 27 Mella

Yania toma de la mano al combatiente
La gloria levanta al compañero
Que no traiciona amigos ni ideales

ANA JOSEFA BREA
        Matías Ramón Mella's wife
Untiring collaborator in the project
        for liberation
In Cuba lives one of her offspring / Born of her lineage
Fighting against tyranny and dying

In Moca in her house made of palm
        a humble beautiful house
Keeping count of the heroic deeds
Lives Matilde Mella / Blind
Almost a century old
She endures disasters
The respect of her people surrounds her
She is the granddaughter of Mella
Driving force of the battle
Great in the uprising
        of the 27th Mella

Yania takes the hand of the fighter
The promise of victory inspires her compañero
Who does not betray his friends or his ideals

Benemérito paladín de las acciones
Matías Ramón en el delirio
De una patria tan pura y grande patria
Que coronan cañones / alabardas

Matías Ramón
Macho del trabucazo
Que grande compañera Ana Josefa Brea
Que vanidad sublime el rostro de Matilde
Cuando recuerda
                las gestas del abuelo

HAY QUE BATIR LAS PALMAS / ALFOMBRAR DE VERDADES EL HEROISMO / VER LLEGAR A JOSEFA ANTONIA DE LA PAZ-CHEPITA LA MADRE DE JUAN ISIDRO PEREZ / LA CALLE DEL ARQUILLO / GUARDA SU CASA FRENTE AL CARMEN / UN 16 DE JULIO NACE LA TRINITARIA / SU CASA ES PUNTO Y FUEGO / DE IDEAS MUY CONCRETAS / LA CONFIDENTE DE LIBERTADORES / CHEPITA PEREZ / TAMBIEN ES TRINITARIA.

Worthy champion of action
Matías Ramón in the delirium
Of a country so pure and a great homeland
Crowned by cannons / broad axes

Matías Ramón
Hero in the uprising
What a close compañera Ana Josefa Brea
What sublime pride in Matilde's face
When she remembers
                    her grandfather's great deeds

WE MUST CLAP OUR HANDS / SHOWER HEROISM WITH TRUTHS / WATCH JOSEFA ANTONIA DE LA PAZ-CHEPITA THE MOTHER OF JUAN ISIDRO PEREZ ARRIVE / ARQUILLO STREET / SHE MAKES HER HOME ACROSS FROM EL CARMEN / ONE 16 OF JULY THE TRINITARIAN WOMAN IS BORN / HER HOUSE IS GROUND ZERO / FOR VERY CONCRETE IDEAS / THE CONFIDANT OF LIBERATORS / CHEPITA PEREZ / SHE IS ALSO A TRINITARIAN.

EL COJITO COMIENZA A MONDAR UNA FRUTA CON LAS MANOS / ESTO ES raro ES raro DICE / MODELANDO LA erre HASTA QUE SE LA enrosca EN LA LENGUA / pero QUE NO SEPAN CUANTAS VECES HAN OCUPADO A YANIA / raro MUY raro / ES SUMAMENTE desconcertante QUE NADIE HABLE DE entregas / CAMINAN apresuradamente ASCIENDEN A grandes ZANCADAS LA EMPINADA CALLE / EL COJITO SE DETIENE EN EL ULTIMO recodo / regresa AL PUNTO DE partida / quieren volver A sacrificar A ESTA DAMA / EL SOL CAE APLASTADO sobre EL mar / APLASTADO por SU propio PESO / AHI LLEGA otra NAVE CON turistas QUE pretenden FILMAR LA crucifixión de Yania López / QUE PELICULA cabrones / DEJAN caer PEDAZOS DE risas / EL COJITO CONTIENE LA respiración / UN CONO DE MONTAÑA SE ELEVA HACIA EL CIELO / por UN COSTADO ASCIENDE rectamente EL mar / COMO SI HUBIERA SIDO TAJADO por UNA POTENCIA DEMENTE / HACIA LA CIMA SE encuentra LA ALDEA DE YANIA / TABLONES TOSCOS Y TECHO DE YAGUA / hambre / hombre / historia DE SUCESOS / ocurridos / corre UN SUAVE SOPLO DE muerte preparada DE tragedia / muerte criticada / arrastrada por GESTOS soberbios / muerte MEZQUINA / MANSA O LOCA / protagonista DE LOS dramas / COMO COSA AJENA AL argumento / EL SOL acaricia LOS PICOS DE LAS MONTAÑAS JUBILOSAS / ahora LA BOCA DEL LEON ESTA EN EL PONIENTE / CON DOS LENGUAS DE tierra proyectadas / LAS BOCAS detrás de LINEAS fronterizas / CON DOS SILUETAS COMPLETAMENTE DISTINTAS sobre UN MISMO vientre DEFINIDAS.

THE CRIPPLE BEGINS TO PEEL A FRUIT WITH HIS
FINGERS / THIS IS rare IT'S rare HE SAYS / TRILLING HIS
r UNTIL IT rolls OFF HIS TONGUE / but HOW CAN THEY
NOT KNOW HOW MANY TIMES THEY HAVE OCCU-
PIED YANIA / strange VERY strange / IT'S VERY disturbing
THAT NO ONE TALKS ABOUT surrender / THEY WALK
fast TAKING long STRIDES THEY GO UP THE STEEP
STREET / THE CRIPPLE STOPS AT THE LAST bend / he
returns TO THE starting POINT / they want TO sacrifice THIS
LADY again / THE SUN FALLS CRUSHED against THE sea /
CRUSHED under ITS own WEIGHT / THERE COMES
another SHIP WITH tourists WHO try TO FILM THE crucifix-
ion of Yania López / WHAT A FILM the fuckers / THEY LET
out BITS OF laughter / THE CRIPPLE HOLDS HIS
breath / A MOUNTAIN PEAK RISES TOWARD THE SKY /
on ONE SIDE THE sea RISES straight up / AS IF
IT HAD BEEN SLASHED by A DEMENTED FORCE /
TOWARD THE PEAK is THE VILLAGE OF YANIA /
ROUGH PLANKS AND A ROOF MADE OF PALM HEMP /
hunger / man / history of EVENTS / taken place / A SOFT
BREEZE OF death made OF tragedy blows / death criticized /
dragged around by arrogant EXPLOITS / STINGY death /
TAME OR MAD / protagonist OF THE dramas / LIKE
SOMETHING FOREIGN TO THE plot / THE SUN caresses
THE PEAKS OF THE LOFTY MOUNTAINS / now THE
LION'S MOUTH IS IN THE WEST / WITH TWO
TONGUES OF land projected / THE MOUTHS behind
TOUCHING BORDERS / WITH TWO COMPLETELY
DIFFERENT SILHOUETTES OUTLINED on THE SAME
womb.

ROSA y su amado Tomás de la Concha
Hacen balas para
La Libertad
Dolores la madre de Tomás muere
    frente
      al cadáver
        del hijo
          fusilado

María-Ana-Mariana
Luisa
Las Pina
Las Bonilla
Las del Monte
Francisca de la Concha
Fusiladas o no
Esas mujeres caminan a paso acelerado
Conscientes de su entrega a un ideal
Mimita Bustamante / La amante de la causa
       Confianza de la causa
Se esconde Francisco del Rosario Sánchez
       En la casa de Pancha
       Pancha López lo cuida
       Junto a los Trinitarios
       Que simulan
       De Francisco el entierro

ROSA and her lover Tomás de la Concha
Make bullets for
Freedom
Dolores the mother of Tomás dies
    upon seeing
        the body
            of her executed
                son

María-Ana-Mariana
Luisa
The Pina women
The Bonilla women
The del Monte women
Francisca de la Concha
Executed or not
Those women are moving quickly
Conscious of their devotion to an ideal
Mimita Bustamante / Lover of the cause
      Confidence of the cause
Francisco del Rosario Sánchez hides
      In Pancha's house
      Pancha López takes care of him
      Along with the Trinitarians
      Who act out
      Francisco's burial

FILOMENA GOMEZ
     trae el arbolito
La flor distintivo Jazmín de Malabar
     para los Trinitarios
La flor que cultivan Manuela / Rosa y
       sus hermanas

Filomena en la lucha con Rosa
María del Carmen Bustamante
Juana Hernández
Juliana Benítez
Ana María Pinzón
Rosario Guillén Alfau
María Baltazara de los Reyes
Centinela / custodia / esconde a
       Juan Pablo
fiel a la campaña del Patricio
     "se arma / acaudilla"
Exalta a los soldados en la contienda

FILOMENA GOMEZ
     brings the young tree
The distinctive flower of the Malabar Jasmine
    for the Trinitarians
The flower cultivated by Manuela / Rosa and
          her sisters

Filomena in the struggle with Rosa
María del Carmen Bustamante
Juana Hernández
Juliana Benítez
Ana María Pinzón
Rosario Guillén Alfau
María Baltazara de los Reyes
Sentry / guard / she hides
      Juan Pablo
faithful to the Patriot's campaign
   "she arms herself / she leads"
She praises the combatants in the conflict

LA noche de la cita
De honor en el Baluarte
Con la bandera de la cruz y cuadros
Concepción Bona abraza / Entrega el pabellón a
      Rosa
           Rosa la espera en
           el Baluarte

Allí María Trinidad con pólvora
                su amplia falda llena
Lucha con todos los patriotas
                      la noche de Febrero

Ana Valverde restaura la Muralla
Con las Duarte / Fue expulsada con ellas

Todas fabrican balas / trajes y vendajes
Todas esas mujeres febreristas
Dios / Patria / y Libertad sus cuerpos
A la inmortalidad
También son Trinitarias

THE night of the appointment
With honor at the Stockade
With the flag bearing four squares and a cross
Concepción Bona embraces / Hands over the banner to
      Rosa
           Rosa waits for her in
           the Stockade

There María Trinidad fills her full skirt
                      with gunpowder
She fights together with all the patriots
                        that February night

Ana Valverde rebuilds the Wall
Together with the Duarte sisters / She was exiled

They all make bullets / uniforms and bandages
All those febreristas
God / Homeland / and Freedom their bodies
To immortality
They are also Trinitarians

Días negros / pasan mujeres / días negros /
pasar mujeres

EL COJITO ABARCA EL AMPLIO PANORAMA DE LA
GUERRA Y LA MUERTE / VE DONDE EL AMOR DE LAS
MUJERES POR SU PATRIA SE DA COMO EL RIO QUE SE
SUICIDA CONFUNDIDO EN EL MAR / O DONDE LAS
FLACAS FUERZAS AL GALOPE SE LEVANTAN PARA
SIEMPRE / MIRANDO SORPRENDIDAS EL NEGRO DE
LAS ARREMETIDAS

Dark days / women pass / dark days
pass women

THE CRIPPLE SURVEYS THE WIDE PANORAMA OF WAR
AND DEATH / HE SEES WHERE THE LOVE OF THE
WOMEN FOR THEIR HOMELAND IS POURED OUT LIKE
THE RIVER THAT IS LOST TO THE SEA, A SUICIDE / OR
WHERE THE FALTERING TROOPS RISE UP GALLOPING
FOREVER / SHOCKED TO SEE THE DESOLATION LEFT
BY THE ATTACKS

EN MOCA

> María Francisca del Monte
> Esposa del General Imbert
> Activa en la campaña

EL 5 DE MARZO DE 1844
ACOMPAÑA AL GENERAL
CUANDO ANUNCIA EN LA PLAZA
LA INDEPENDENCIA NACIONAL

IN MOCA

        María Francisca del Monte
        Wife of General Imbert
        Active in the campaign

ON 5 MARCH 1844
SHE IS WITH THE GENERAL
IN THE PLAZA WHEN HE DECLARES
NATIONAL INDEPENDENCE

EN LA VEGA

        María del Carmen
        Angustia
        Manuela y
        Francisca Villa

EL 4 DE MARZO DE 1844
EN LA VEGA IZAN LA BANDERA
DE LA PATRIA / BORDADA POR
LAS HERMANAS VILLA

Después / invitado JUAN PABLO
Pasa cinco días en la casa de María /
Angustia / Manuela y Francisca Villa

IN LA VEGA

        María del Carmen
        Angustia
        Manuela and
        Francisca Villa

ON 4 MARCH 1844
IN LA VEGA THEY HOIST THE FLAG
OF THE NATION / SEWN BY
THE VILLA SISTERS

Afterwards / JUAN PABLO as a guest
Spends five days in María's house /
Angustia / Manuela and Francisca Villa

JUANA GAU
Mujer de Montellanos / Guerrillera
Lucha con ímpetu en la Batalla de
                Sabana Larga

JUANA SALTITOPA / Con vocación para los
                    lances
Con la gente de Marco Trinidad
Se une a la acción bélica de los libertadores
            del 30 de Marzo
            estimula la lucha
            cruza el río entre balas
            regresa con el agua necesaria
            para que no se fundan los cañones
Junto a los grandes héroes / Lucha la guerrillera
Popular Coronela / Heroína por la Patria y
            nosotros
Yania llora el injusto tratamiento
Los reproches con que se la recuerda

ROSA MONTAS se indigna al paso de
                  invasores
No abandona a su esposo Duvergé
Centinela de fuego en la Frontera

JUANA GAU
Of Montellanos / Guerrilla fighter
Fights courageously in the Battle of
                Sabana Larga

JUANA SALTITOPA / With a skill for handling
                        difficult situations
With the people of Marco Trinidad
She joins the fighting of the liberators
        of 30 March
           she urges on the fighting
           crosses the river dodging bullets
           returns with much-needed water
           to keep the cannons from melting down
Along with the great heroes / The female warrior fights
A Beloved Colonel / Heroine of the Nation and
           us
Yania laments the unjust treatment
The reproaches by which she is remembered

ROSA MONTAS is outraged at the march of
                invaders
She does not abandon her husband Duvergé
Armed sentry on the Border

MICAELA RIVERA
Viuda de Miguel Febles
Se casa de nuevo
Entrega su Hato al esposo
El General Pedro Santana
Casa Froilana Febles / hija de Micaela
Con Ramón / el hermano de Pedro

CLEOFES VALDEZ de Mota se violenta frente al
                                esposo fusilado
Rompe en canto de llanto
                      la venta de la Patria
                                por Santana

Cuánto amor de mujeres por su tierra

MICAELA RIVERA
Widow of Miguel Febles
Remarries
She hands over her Ranch to her husband
General Pedro Santana
She marries off her daughter / Froilana Febles
To Ramón / Pedro's brother

CLEOFES VALDEZ de Mota becomes violently enraged as she
                               watches her husband executed
She bursts into a wailing chant
                       the selling of the Nation
                                     by Santana

How great is the women's love for their land

MANUELA MOTA antianexionista
Acusa a su padre en Baní / La entrega la
                    enloquece

ENCARNACION VILLASECA DEL MONTE
                    da la espalda al traidor

JOSEFA ANTONIA DEL MONTE reprocha de
        "Eugenio la sangre derramada"

Llenas de espanto
Balbina Peña y
María Socorro Sánchez exclaman

            "EL CRIMEN ES LA VENTA DE LA
            PATRIA
            LA REPUBLICA VENDIDA AL
            EXTRANJERO".

MANUELA MOTA antiannexationist
Denounces her father in Baní / The betrayal
                              drives her mad

ENCARNACION VILLASECA DEL MONTE
                          turns her back on the traitor

JOSEFA ANTONIA DEL MONTE reproaches for
            "Eugenio the blood spilled"

Full of fear
Balbina Peña and
María Socorro Sánchez exclaim

                "THE CRIME IS THE SELLING OF THE
                NATION
                THE REPUBLIC SOLD TO THE
                FOREIGNER."

NO SE RINDEN / ALERTA EL COJITO / NO SUENAN CLARINES / NO SE RINDEN / UN GRAN SILENCIO DOMINA EN LAS LINEAS Y EN LOS CAMPAMENTOS EL CONTINUO TRONAR DE LOS PLOMOS / GRITA INDIGNADO / PEDRO VENTA / VARIOS PASOS ATRAS / PEDRO MATARILE / LIRE / ESE HOMBRE QUE NOS VENDE ES UNA VAINA / LAS MUJERES CONTINUAN LA MARCHA / SE ENCUENTRAN CON ESE SUCESO NEGRO / CON LA LINEA NEGRA / SOBRE ESTA SE PUDREN CUERPOS DE SACRIFICADOS / AUN QUEDAN LOS RUGIDOS / CUERPOS QUE PIDEN SU BANDERA / DONDE MUERE UN CAMINO / QUEDA MUERTO UN ENEMIGO DEL TRAIDOR

THEY REFUSE TO SURRENDER / WARNS THE CRIPPLE / THE TRUMPETS AREN'T SOUNDING / THEY'RE NOT SURRENDERING / A GREAT SILENCE REIGNS OVER THE LINES AND IN THE CAMPS THE CONSTANT THUNDER OF SHELLS / HE SHOUTS INDIGNANTLY / PEDRO VENTA / SEVERAL STEPS BEHIND / PEDRO MATARILE / LIRE / THAT MAN WHO IS SELLING US OUT IS A PIG / THE WOMEN CONTINUE THE MARCH / THEY COME UPON THAT HORRIBLE SIGHT / THE HORRIBLE LINE / WHERE THE BODIES OF THE SACRIFICED LIE ROTTING / THEIR CRIES CAN STILL BE HEARD / BODIES ASKING FOR THEIR FLAG / AT THE END OF EVERY ROAD / AN ENEMY OF THE TRAITOR IS LEFT DEAD

ESTO SERA PAIS PERO
NUNCA NACION / DICE
A SU HIJO FRANCISCO
DEL ROSARIO

SANCHEZ

Su padre
NARCISO

THIS WILL BE A COUNTRY BUT
NEVER A NATION / SAYS
TO HIS SON FRANCISCO
DEL ROSARIO

SANCHEZ

His father
NARCISO

A grandes mujeres exalta
Josefa Perdomo
> "Ahí Trinidad Sánchez, la valiente
> Los guerreros animan la batalla
> Ana Valverde con su celo ardiente
> Reedifica más tarde la Muralla
> Pero entre todo brilla
> Por su valor, la heroica Baltazara
> Baltazara la grande, la sin par,
> Se arma, corre, las huestes acaudilla,
> Y a luchar con denuedo se prepara".

LA POLITICA NO ES UNA ESPECULACION / REPITE EL COJITO / LEYENDO EL IDEARIO DEL HERMANO DE ROSA / AHI LLEGA OTRO GRUPO TRIUNFANTE / EL VALOR / LA LIRA / LA FILOSOFIA

ROSA repite de su hermano JUAN PABLO
"El crimen no prescribe ni queda impune"

Josefa Perdomo
Praises great women
>"Behold Trinidad Sánchez, the brave one,
>The fighters keep the battle alive
>Ana Valverde with her burning zeal
>Later rebuilds the Wall
>But in the midst of everything outstanding
>For her bravery, the heroic Baltazara
>Baltazara the great, the unrivaled,
>Arms herself, runs, rallies the troops
>And prepares herself to fight courageously."

POLITICS IS NOT MERE SPECULATION / SAYS THE CRIPPLE OVER AND OVER / READING THE MANIFESTO OF ROSA'S BROTHER / THERE COMES ANOTHER VICTORIOUS UNIT / BRAVERY / THE LIRE / PHILOSOPHY

ROSA repeats the words of her brother JUAN PABLO
"Crime does not rule nor will it go unpunished"

Salomé Ureña / más tarde / defraudada
Quiebra el silencio impuesto
Frente al Decreto de la Ley Marcial
Que interpreta el tirano Lilís

           "Hace ya tanto tiempo. Silenciosa
           si indiferente no, Patria Bendita,
           yo he seguido la lucha fatigosa
           con que llevas de bien tu alma infinita.
           Ha tiempo que no llena
           Tus confines la voz de mi esperanza,
           ni el alma que contigo se enajena
           a señalarte el porvenir se lanza".

        Pasándose la mano
          Por el verde cabello / Tú Yania queda a
                                 salvo
Mirando sorprendida un puente sobre un
               profundo abismo
Lo que queda / nunca será perdido ni el mundo
                      de mañana

Salomé Ureña / later / feeling cheated
Breaks the silence imposed
In defiance of the Martial Law Decree
Which the tyrant Lilís interprets

      "For a long time now. Silent
      but not indifferent, Glorious Nation,
      I have followed the course of the consuming
      battle with which you satisfy your infinite
      soul. It's been a long time since the voice
      of my hope has filled Your horizons,
      or since my soul estranged from you
      has set out to show you the future."

      Running your hand
      Through your green hair / You Yania are
                          safe
Surprised as she watches a bridge over a
                    deep ravine
What remains today / will never be lost nor will the world
                                      of tomorrow

OTRO GRUPO TRIUNFANTE / EL VALOR / LA LIRA / LA FILOSOFIA

POR la Patria y por todos
Sin fábulas de cantos ni de asombros
Su voz / aquel clamor de mando
Con sus ecos sensatos
Trasmiten la enseñanza
         sobre el terso cordaje
         de la sabiduría
         por su amor y su honra
         a la Patria de Duarte de Sánchez de
         Mella
La voz de las maestras / Llegan al sacrificio
Enseñan Historia Patria / La Moral y la Cívica
Llenan el alma cual si vivieran
               luces
               sin un descanso apenas
La enseñanza / La alborada / Cada gesto pronunciado
                             inteligentemente
Y la fe sin las lanzas penetra la cultura
La luz se fija en
         María Nicolasa Billini
         Anacaona Moscoso
         Juana Dolores Gómez

ANOTHER TRIUMPHANT UNIT / BRAVERY / THE LYRE / PHILOSOPHY

FOR the Nation and for everyone
Without ceremony
Their voice / that cry of command
With its echoes of wisdom
They pass on their teaching
           on the clear strings
           of knowledge
           for love and honor
           for the Nation of Duarte of Sánchez of
           Mella
The voice of the teachers / They come to sacrifice themselves
They teach National History / Ethics and Civics
They fill the soul as if they were living
           lights
           with scarcely any rest
The teaching / The dawn / Each expression pronounced
           intelligently
Faith without swords permeates the culture
The light shines on
        María Nicolasa Billini
        Anacaona Moscoso
        Juana Dolores Gómez

Antera Mota
Rosa Sméster
Maestras cual un faro / Dan con su voz el ejemplo /
El sacrificio llena espacios necesarios /
Escribimos más nombres
Leonor Feltz
Luisa Ozema Pellerano
Ana Josefa Puello
Mercedes Laura Aguiar
Abigaíl Mejía

La Ciencia y la Cultura coronan a
Evangelina Rodríguez
Cesan la soledad y el desconsuelo
Da su ciencia con tanto amor al pobre
Que la fiel pulsación de sus arterias
Le lastiman las sienes y la espantan

                    Antera Mota
                    Rosa Sméster
Teachers like a beacon / Set the example with their voice /
Sacrifice fills the necessary spaces /
                    We write more names
                            Leonor Feltz
                            Luisa Ozema Pellerano
                            Ana Josefa Puello
                            Mercedes Laura Aguiar
                            Abigaíl Mejía

Science and Culture crown
Evangelina Rodríguez
Solitude and grief cease
She offers her knowledge with so much love for the poor
That the constant throbbing of her arteries
Pounds her temples and frightens her

Flérida de Nolasco / Siempre desvelada
                    su seriedad de vida
Trasmite la cultura
Un quehacer la devora
Da la investigación
En cada pentagrama recoge una enseñanza
En cada poesía se mira frente a frente
La desata / Se hace un sitio grande
                    En nuestra historia triste

Flérida de Nolasco / Her seriousness for life
always alert
She spreads culture
A task consumes her
She researches
In every pentagram she finds a lesson
In every poem she challenges herself
It frees her / A great place is made
In our sad history

1916 / SOBRE la Mar Caribe / Aquí está el invasor
Justo a diez metros del casco colonial
Ensaya el pez de acero
El Memphis / los marinos
La bota cruel del gringo
El águila y su poder rapaz
Oh Yania tristeza tuya triste
Las cárceles están llenas
Ahogan / no ahogan / no triunfarán
La tierra es Yania López
abandera los símbolos

**"QUE QUISQUEYA SERA DESTRUIDA
  PERO SIERVA POR SIEMPRE
  JAMAS"**

EN SANTIAGO / se indigna por la audaz
                              ocupación
Ercilia Pepín
        Levanta su voz en la Campaña
        contra los invasores

Más tarde frente a los cadáveres de los
Perozo desafía al tirano
Con bandera de luto

1916 / ON the Caribbean Sea / Behold the invader
Just ten meters from the colonial center
The fish of steel rehearses
The Memphis / the marines
The cruel boot of the gringo
The eagle and its rapacious power
Oh Yania your sad sorrow
The prisons are full
They're drowning / they're not drowning / they will not triumph
The land is Yania López
she champions the symbols

"THAT QUISQUEYA MAY BE DESTROYED
        BUT SERVANT FOREVER
        NEVER"

IN SANTIAGO / indignant about the insolent
                              occupation
Ercilia Pepín
      Raises her voice in the Campaign
      against the invaders

Later seeing the bodies of the
Perozos she defies the tyrant
With a banner of mourning

EN EL ESTE / SECUNDINA REYES / La Cacica
La guerrillera acosa a los del Norte
                que bajan la bandera
                toman la tierra nuestra
                levantan monopolios
                      de caña
                      de azúcar
                      se quedan oprimen
                      explotan   se quedan
                                  se quedan
                                  se quedan

Al igual que un hombre
                en las revoluciones
En la Línea Noroeste
CEFERINA CALDERON es un valiente ejemplo
En las comarcas donde la Paz reclama
CASILDA CRESPO con el fusil al hombro
Hace causa con los defensores

Aunque los vivos reposen en sus lechos
El ojo del terror vela

IN THE EAST / SECUNDINA REYES / The Leader
The revolutionary hunts down those from the North
              who lower the flag
              seize our land
              set up monopolies
                    of cane
                    of sugar
                    they stay they oppress
                    they exploit   they stay
                          they stay
                      they stay

Like a man
        in a revolution
On the Northeast Front
CEFERINA CALDERON is a brave example
In the regions where Peace resounds
CASILDA CRESPO with her rifle on her shoulder
Takes up the cause of the defenders

Although the living may be resting in their beds
A terrified eye keeps watch

TRINA MOYA DE VASQUEZ / Primera Dama
    Dama sin prepotencia
Grande y humilde dama
    glorifica a las madres
    "Venid los moradores
    del campo a la ciudad
    entonemos un himno
    de intenso amor filial".

CANTAN A LAS MIRABAL

Estaba Minerva? Estaba
Estaba Patria?   Estaba
Estaba María Teresa? Estaba

Estaban las Mirabal
Encendido en cada pecho
   el dolor / la cruz
Chorro de sangre los ojos
Lágrimas de tantos huesos
Cenizas de tantos muertos bajaban
Por sus tres caras

TRINA MOYA DE VÁSQUEZ / First Lady
                Lady without much power
Great and humble lady
            glorifies the mothers
            "Come residents
            from the country to the city
            let us strike up a hymn
            of intense sisterly love."

THEY SING TO THE MIRABAL SISTERS

Was Minerva there?   She was
Was Patria there?   She was
Was María Teresa there?   She was

The Mirabal sisters were there
Each breast burning with
        the pain / the cross
Their eyes a stream of blood
Tears from so many bones
Ashes from so many dead rolled
Down their three faces

Era sangre de los mártires
        callados por el terror
        y la muerte

Las tres amaban la Patria
        el tambor / la libertad
Las tres rodaron / cada una
        era bandera
Una bandera muy grande
que aprisionaba sus cuerpos
        con la carne destrozada

Donde flotan las banderas
Lloran por la libertad Minerva / Patria / María Teresa
"Que bellas en el tope" están
Las hijas de Doña Chea
Madre de las Mirabal

It was the blood of martyrs
            silenced by terror
            and death

The three loved their Nation
            the drum / freedom
The three were murdered / each one
            was a banner
A huge banner
that wrapped their bodies
            together with their torn flesh

Wherever the flags fly
Minerva / Patria / María Teresa cry for freedom
"How beautiful on the flagpole" they are
The daughters of Doña Chea
Mother of the Mirabal sisters

LUPERON — Julio 14 del 49
Constanza / Maimón / Estero Hondo — Junio 14 del 59
La Manacla — Diciembre 23 año 63
Revolución de Abril — 24 del 65
Caracoles — Febrero 6 del 73

FEFITA JUSTO TAVAREZ — ANGELA RICART — GUILLERMINA PUIGSUBIRA — ESTELA MICHEL — MARIA FAXAS Y TANTAS OTRAS NOBLES DAMAS LACERADAS POR PREMATURAS MUERTES DE SUS HIJOS GLORIOSOS

LUPERON — July 14 of 49
Constanza / Maimón / Estero Hondo — June 14 of 59
La Manacla — December 23 year 63
Revolution of April — 24 of 65
Caracoles — February 6 of 73

FEFITA JUSTO TAVAREZ — ANGELA RICART — GUILLERMINA PUIGSUBIRA — ESTELA MICHEL — MARIA FAXAS AND SO MANY OTHER NOBLE WOMEN PIERCED TO THE QUICK BY THE PREMATURE DEATHS OF THEIR GLORIOUS SONS

CARMEN NATALIA canta
    "¡Adelante, soldado del rescate!
    Beso tu mano así cerrada
    Sobre un fusil que no está hecho
        a la medida
    de tu mano pacífica y amable
    Ahí, frente a los brutos, mi corazón
        está contigo.
    Y mis manos se cierran en tus dedos,
    Y te grito al oído ¡Viva la libertad, hermano!

    En marcha ¡En marcha!
    Todo un pueblo que sufre nos espera.
    En marcha, ya, soldado del rescate,
    inminente y preciso ¡En Marcha! ¡En Marcha!"

MERCEDES MOTA
recaba fondos para la estatua de Duarte

CARMEN NATALIA sings
    "Onward, soldier of rescue!
  I kiss your hand clenched
  On a rifle that isn't made
      to fit
  your peace-loving and kind hand
  There, standing before the savages, my heart
      is with you.
  My hands close around your fingers,
  And I shout in your ear, Long live freedom, brother!

  On your feet Let's move!
  An entire suffering people awaits us.
  Move, now, soldier of rescue,
  imminent and urgent, On Your Feet! Let's Move!

MERCEDES MOTA
raises funds for the statue of Duarte

1965   Después de treintiún años cumplidos
De férrea tiranía
El pueblo reclama la Ley Sustantiva /
Para salvar vidas
        Falsedad cruel y vil
Vuelve la yankihorda
Se instala sobre Yania
Rueda / No rueda la determinación
Tres millones dicen NO
Habría que matar hasta el último hombre
        decente de la mitad de la Isla

EN las Montañas Jubilosas
Donde nace la luz de las auroras
. Los coros de mujeres se repiten
        "Ningún pueblo ser libre merece
        Si es esclavo / indolente y servil"

1965 After thirty-one years
   Of iron-fisted tyranny
   The people reclaim the Substantive Law /
   To save lives
     Cruel and vile lie
   The yankeehoard returns
   Settles down on Yania
   It takes hold / Their master plan does not take hold
   Three million say NO
   They would have to kill every last decent man
     on this half of the Island

     IN the Lofty Mountains
     Where the dawn's light is born
     The women's choruses are repeated
       "No nation deserves to be free
       If enslaved / indolent and servile"

YOLANDA GUZMAN delegada barrial
Lucha en la Revolución de Abril
         Aquí está el invasor
Yolanda asesinada
Los hijos del pueblo levantan a su heroína
Yolanda / asesinada

OH tiempo sin los cambios / Siempre lo inalcanzable
La mujer que se ofrece / FLORINDA SORIANO
Mamá Tingó acribillada
Por las botas del amo

La tan nombrada Yania López
Por todas sus tragedias tristes
Oh Yania / Oh Tierra / Reconoce a Florinda
         asesinada
           en defensa del hombre
           explotado

HILDA GAUTREAUX / luchadora
jurista / busca en la Justicia
              la Justicia
La bomba uniformada la destroza

YOLANDA GUZMAN neighborhood representative
Fights in the April Revolution
              The invader is here
Yolanda murdered
The children of the nation raise up their heroine
Yolanda / murdered

OH unchanging times / Always the unattainable
The woman who volunteers / FLORINDA SORIANO
Mamá Tingó trampled
Under the boots of the master

The often beseeched Yania López
For all her sad tragedies
Oh Yania / Oh Nation / She recognizes Florinda
              murdered
              defending the
              exploited

HILDA GAUTREAUX / fighter
lawyer / searches for Justice in
                        Justice
The uniformed bomb destroys her

AMELIA
RICART
CALVENTI / Escolar que aprende y
    enseña
    el deber de luchar / cae / muere

        HONESTA / tan perfecta
        En el amor tan grande / DOÑA CHUCHA
        Que el corazón de grande repartido
        Da para cada niño abandonado / que recoge y
            alberga
            esta mujer del
            pueblo

AY / quién se rie sin quererlo
Veraz y auténtico destino
En el jardín la flor tan escogida
De pie también sembrada
Se seca por la sangre derramada
Se niega a adornar los salones
De los devastadores de la Patria

AMELIA
RICART
CALVENTI / A scholar who learns and
    teaches
       the duty of fighting / falls / dies

        HONEST / so perfect
        Out of such great love / DOÑA CHUCHA
        From her heart a big share
        Is given to each abandoned child / whom she
                        gathers to her and
                  shelters
                  this woman of the
                  people

AY / who is laughing thoughtlessly
True and undisputed destiny
In the garden the chosen flower
Planted tall and upright
Dries up from all the blood spilled
Refuses to adorn the halls
Of the Nation's ravagers

DICE EL COJITO A MANUELA / A OLAYA / A MIMITA /
A CHEPITA / A FILOMENA / QUE VIAJA Y ENTREGA LA
FLOR DE MALABAR / INSIGNIA DE LA CAUSA
TRINITARIA / LO MAS PENOSO ES LA HISTORIA DE LA
CORRUPCION QUE ENGENDRA EL PODER / Y LO
ASOMBROSO / QUE TODAS ESAS COSAS OCURREN
REALMENTE COMO LO ESCRIBE CLAUDIO EN ROMA

El tonto aún suena los nudillos de los dedos
Los amigos toman café en desportilladas jarras

EL COJITO / VOIME A MORIR DE AMOR DE PENA /
POR NO HABER VISTO OTRA MANERA / TIRANOS /
DICTADORES / DEPREDADORES / LAGRIMAS
NEGRAS EN TODAS DIRECCIONES / MUERTOS
HEROES Y MARTIRES

THE CRIPPLE SAYS TO MANUELA / TO OLAYA / TO
MIMITA / TO CHEPITA / TO FILOMENA / WHO TRAV-
ELS AND DELIVERS THE FLOWER OF MALABAR /
EMBLEM OF THE TRINITARIAN CAUSE / THE MOST
PAINFUL THING IS THE HISTORY OF CORRUPTION
THAT IS BRED BY POWER / AND THE ASTONISHING
THING / THAT ALL THESE THINGS HAPPEN JUST AS
CLAUDIUS WRITES ABOUT THEM IN ANCIENT ROME

The idiot still cracks his knuckles
His friends drink coffee from cracked mugs

THE CRIPPLE / I'M GONNA DIE OF LOVE OF
SORROW / BECAUSE I HAVEN'T SEEN ANY OTHER
WAY / TYRANTS / DICTATORS / PILLAGERS /
TEARS OF RAGE EVERYWHERE / DEAD HEROES
AND MARTYRS

AQUI traiciones entre banderas
                              negras
Y relojes que marcan las edades
La historia / Comienza en Marién
            Diciembre 25
            92 del 400
Ciento ochenta y dos mil
            quinientos días
            contando los bisiestos
A doce años para el gran HAPPY BIRTHDAY
            al pie de Cinco Siglos

DESDE entonces
En las Montañas Jubilosas
Se rompe el cielo / Cae a pedazos
Baja la lluvia / pura sangre baja amarga
                              la lluvia
                              baja
                              sangre

HERE lie betrayals among blackened
                              flags
And clocks that mark the ages
History / Begins in Marién
              December 25
              92 of 400
One hundred eighty two thousand
              five hundred days
              counting the leap years
Twelve years until the big HAPPY BIRTHDAY
              at the end of Five Centuries

SINCE then
In the Lofty Mountains
The sky breaks / Falls in pieces
The rain comes down / pure blood comes down bitter
                              rain
                              comes down as
                              blood

SALEN / salen historias que parecen mancas
Prendidas a la piel con alfileres
Sonido
Olfato
Lágrima
Y la degustación a plomo puro
Salen historias como partos / Salen
Con aureola de placenta agria
Llegan aún del Norte / Los piratas saquean
La riqueza del café / azúcar / cacao
oro / plata / níquel / la bauxita

Y el hambre mata al hombre
Caen y se levantan muertos
Sin el toque personal de algún delito

YANIA se desconcierta del juego y las apuestas
Con el cordón umbilical atado
El macho que rechaza
Es devuelto con retrato de esqueleto
Sin derroche / tan cierto
Que su estirpe respetan las Manuela
Las Olaya las Josefa
Es la Historia / Luto negro

THEY COME / stories come that look deformed
Attached to the skin with pins
Sounds
Smells
Tears
The taste of pure lead
Stories come like births / They come
With an aroma of sour placenta
They keep coming from the North / The pirates loot
Riches from coffee / sugar / cacao
gold / silver / nickel / bauxite

Hunger kills man
The dead fall and rise up
Not because of some petty crime

YANIA is disconcerted by the game and the stakes
With his umbilical cord attached
The man who fights back
Is returned a skeleton
No waste / so certain
That his offspring will respect the Manuelas
The Olayas the Josefas
It is History / A black mourning

GRITA EL COJITO CON ALEGRIA Y PENA
INDIAS / NEGRAS / BLANCAS / MESTIZAS /
MULATAS / LAS AMAN LA JUSTICIA Y EL
AMOR CON RESPETO ¡VENID!

¡Ea! ¡Mujeres!
¡Ea! ¡Mujeres!

¡Soltad los pájaros de la esperanza!
¡Ea! ¡Mujeres!
¡Soltad Palomas!

THE CRIPPLE CRIES WITH JOY AND SORROW /
INDIAN WOMEN / BLACK WOMEN / WHITE WOMEN /
MESTIZA WOMEN / MULATTA WOMEN / JUSTICE AND
LOVE LOVE THEM WITH RESPECT COME!

        Come on! Women!
        Come on! Women!

      Release the birds of hope!
        Come on! Women!
            Release the Doves!

NOTES

Page 51

Line 7: Carlos V, Holy Roman Emperor, also known as Carlos I, King of Spain from 1517 to 1556, was the grandson of Queen Isabel and King Fernando and the heir to the vast domain of the newly conquered lands in the Americas.

Page 57

Line 6: Encomenderos were the original colonials empowered as officials of town councils who received entire communities of indigenous laborers to work for them on the land and in the mines. The labor distribution system was first called repartimiento and later encomienda. This labor contributed to the riches shared by the colonizers, and abuse of the system was in violation of the royal order to respect the indigenous population. In 1501 the Crown declared that the indigenous citizens were free vassals and that they should not be treated badly, but in 1503 Commander Ovando persuaded Queen Isabel to rescind that policy, arguing that if she did not force the indigenous to work the mines, the island would lose its population and its wealth.

Line 16: Tower of Homage (Torre del Homenaje) was built by indigenous labor during the Conquest / Colonial period as part of the Fortress in Santo Domingo and was used in the 1844 Independence movement to imprison the revolutionaries.

Page 59

Line 9 & 10: The yucca and the guáyiga were important plants used for food in the Taíno society. The yucca was used to make casabe, "the bread of the Indies," a staple used by the Spanish and exported throughout the other colonies. The guáyiga is an edible root used by the Taíno.

Line 11: During the colonial period, gold was washed from the rivers by young Taíno women as part of their forced labor obligation under the system of repartimientos and encomiendas.

Page 61

Lines 5 & 6: Enriquillo is the protagonist of the novel, *Enriquillo*, by the Dominican writer Manuel de Jesús Galván. The novel was published in 1882 and was one of the many post-Independence era attempts to retrace colonial history from a modern perspective. Although Galván defended the Spanish conquest, he was critical of the abuses committed against the indigenous population by Governor Nicolás de Ovando and others. His somewhat romanticized account of the colonial period is popularly regarded as authentic. Enriquillo was the Christian name given to Guarocuya, young descendant and successor of one of the caciques of Jaraguá. He was treated as the palace favorite by Viceroy Diego Colón and his wife. He married Mencía, the mestiza daughter of Higüemota and granddaughter of Anacaona. After many attempts to cooperate with the colonizers, Enriquillo led a rebellion of his people and escaped to the mountains where they survived as an independent community.

Page 63

Line 6: Areitos were ritual songs and dances often given as a tribute. They were performed as dances, directed by one who recited the stories and repeated in a louder voice by a dancing chorus, accompanied by a wooden drum. They were used to commemorate events that were worthy of being preserved as a historical or cultural lesson. Their purpose was didactic as well as celebratory, to reinforce the bonds of community between the members of each group through participation in a common history.

Page 69

Lines 7, 8 & 9: The Court of Viceroys included Francisco de

Garay, the Chief Constable of Hispaniola, Francisco de Tostado, Clerk of the High Court, Alonso Dávila, Councilman in charge of the general administration of municipal interests, and Diego Caballero, Secretary of the High Court, all sugar planters and officials who served Diego Colón, the Viceroy of Hispaniola from 1520. Historical accounts indicate that these officials betrayed Viceroy Diego Colón and his humanitarian labor position and worked for their own interests as planters.

Line 11: Father Antonio Montesino was a Dominican priest who took a revolutionary stand against the atrocities to which the Indians were subjected throughout the colony and the cruelty with which the forced labor system was exploited. The conflict was between the official humanitarian position of Viceroy Diego Colón and the economic interests of the sugar planters.

Page 71

Line 13: Teodora and Micaela Ginés were freed slaves who became well-known for their music, the "Son de Ma Teodora" or "La Tonada de la Má Teodora" documented in the poem. They played the bandola and vihuela, instruments which were very common at that time.

Page 75

Line 5: Bartolomé de las Casas, an opponent of Governor Nicolás de Ovando and the sugar planters, was the famous Dominican priest who dedicated his life and work to saving the indigenous population from the atrocities of the conquest. Unfortunately, the solution he suggested to Carlos V was to import Africans as slaves.

Page 81

Line 13: Edith Piaf was a French cabaret singer, the "Voice of Resistance" during the fascist occupation of France in World War II.

Line 14: España Boba, usually translated as Silly Spain or Useless Spain, is the name given to the historical period from 1809 to 1821. Santo Domingo was free from Haitian control and technically a Spanish colony again, but Spain was too weak to support its colonies. Most of the other Spanish colonies throughout Latin America were involved in successful independence movements at this time, but a conservative and ineffective government in Santo Domingo repressed all independence conspiracies there. In 1821, independence from Spain was finally gained with the collaboration of Haitian President Jean-Pierre Boyer. Unfortunately, Boyer's assistance was part of his plan to take control of all the island, incorporated under the new independent government of Haiti. Boyer invaded Santo Domingo in 1822.

Page 83

Line 2: On more than one occasion, the women of Santo Domingo took their jewelry to the Treasury authorities (La Casa del Cordón) to help finance the defense of their city.

Page 85

Lines 5 & 6: Dominga de los Núñez de Cáceres was a respected lady of Santo Domingo who bravely confronted Haitian governor Toussaint L'Ouverture during his occupation of the city in 1801. According to the story, he approached her on the town square and touched her with his cane. She did not hesitate to express her indignation.

Page 89

Lines 10 & 11: Rosa Duarte was exiled to Venezuela with her family for their leadership in the 1844 Independence movement.

Lines 11 & 12: María Trinidad Sánchez was the aunt of revolutionary leader, Francisco del Rosario Sánchez and his sister, Socorro del Rosario Sánchez. She was imprisoned for her opposition to Santana's government and his annexation plan.

Line 14: Balbina Peña was the wife of revolutionary leader, Francisco del Rosario Sánchez. She was imprisoned for her political activities and later exiled to Curaçao.

Page 93
Lines 4, 5, 6, 7, 8 & 9: Mariana Rafaela de la Concha, María Paula and Agueda Bona, the Alfau Bustamante sisters, María Antonia de la Concha and María de Jesús Pina were women from important families, active in the Philanthropic Society and in the Independence movement.

Page 97
Line 1: Pedro Antonio Bobea and Alejandro Pina were playwrights and actors who participated in the Philanthropic Society.

Page 99
Line 7: Manuela Diez y Jiménez Viuda Duarte was the mother of the Duarte family of revolutionaries. Her family had been exiled to Puerto Rico during the years of Haitian invasions. She dedicated her family's money and her own life to the cause of national sovereignty. The flower of the Malabar Jasmine was the symbol of the revolutionary movement, worn by women in their hair and by men on their coats.

Page 101
Line 2: The Trinitarian Society was the secret revolutionary organization formed in 1838 with the purpose of ending the Haitian occupation and establishing national Independence.

Lines 10, 11 & 12: Francisca, Filomena and Sandalia were the sisters of Rosa and Juan Pablo Duarte.

Line 13: María Antonia Bobadilla de Nouel was the daughter

of Ana Valverde. Both were committed revolutionaries and were exiled.

Line 14: Juan Pablo Duarte is regarded as the founder of the independent Dominican Republic. He was inspired by the democratic ideas of his time and by other successful Independence revolutions in the Americas. He dedicated his own education to teaching classes for those who had not had the opportunity for a formal education. He and his fellow revolutionaries, all documented in the poem, organized the Trinitarian Society and led the Revolution.

Line 20: Vicente Celestino was the brother of Rosa and Juan Pablo Duarte, also a revolutionary. He remained in Santo Domingo while his family was exiled and kept them informed. He was assassinated in 1855.

Page 105
Line 2: Francisco del Rosario Sánchez was one of the Trinitarian founders of the independent Dominican Republic.

Line 12: Andrés Sánchez was the brother of revolutionary leader, Francisco del Rosario Sánchez. He was hanged with his aunt María Trinidad Sánchez in 1845 for his opposition to President Santana.

Line 19: Olaya (Olalla) was the mother of the Sánchez family of revolutionaries.

Page 111
Line 2: Matías Ramón Mella was one of the Trinitarian founders of the independent Dominican Republic.

Page 113
Line 12: Josefa Antonia Pérez de la Paz, known as Doña

Chepita, was the mother of revolutionary leader, Juan Isidro Pérez. Her house on Arquillo Street was where the Trinitarian Society was founded on July 16, 1838. Her house is known as the "House where the Dominican Republic was born."

Line 13: Juan Isidro Pérez was one of the Trinitarian founders of the independent Dominican Republic. He was also an actor in the Philanthropic Society.

Page 117
Line 1: Tomás de la Concha was also a Trinitarian.

Line 4: According to the poem, Dolores was the mother of Tomás de la Concha, but according to historian Ferreras, his mother was Marta de la Concha and Dolores was Doña Dolores Hernández Puello who hid Juan Pablo in her home during this time of persecution.

Lines 9, 10, 11, 12, 13, 14 & 18: The Pina women, Alfonsa and Elvira Bonilla, the del Monte women, Francisca de la Concha and Mimita Bustamante were all active women in the 1844 Independence movement. Many women were imprisoned, exiled or executed but faced these dangers without regard for their personal safety.

Page 119
Line 1: Filomena Gómez de Cova returned from exile upon the creation of the Trinitarian Society and brought the Malabar Jasmine. She was the sister of Fernando Gómez, a leader of the Independence movement.

Line 8: María del Carmen Bustamante (Mimita) was the wife / mother of the Alfau Bustamante family of revolutionaries and leaders in the Independence movement. Her son Felipe Alfau Bustamante was a Trinitarian.

Line 9: Juana Hernández was a poet who participated in the Independence movement.

Line 13: María Baltazara de los Reyes armed herself with a rifle and stood guard during "El Grito de Independencia," the night of February 27 and the morning of February 28 when Independence was declared. She was considered the leader of the Febreristas.

Page 125
Line 3: General José María Imbert led troops against the Haitian occupation in the 1844 Independence movement in Moca in the north of the country.

Page 129
Line 1: Juana Gau from Montellanos was undoubtedly Petronila Gau who, as the poem documents, fought in the Independence struggle in the Battle of Sabana Larga.

Line 5: Juana Saltitopa was Juana Trinidad who fought as a revolutionary in the Independence battle at Santiago on March 30, 1844. She was known as "La Coronela."

Line 7: Marco (Marcos) Trinidad was a relative of Juana Saltitopa who commanded troops in the Independence battle at Santiago.

Line 19: Rosa Montás was the wife of General Antonio Duvergé, the governor of Azua on the south coast and commander of troops along the Haitian border during the Independence movement. She fought with him and aided the wounded.

Page 133

Line 1: Manuela Mota was undoubtedly Encarnación "Canela" Mota, daughter of President Manuel de Regla Mota. As the poem documents, she was an antiannexationist who spoke out against her father when he raised the Spanish flag. She was known as "La Heroína Banileja."

Lines 4 & 6: Encarnación Villaseca del Monte and Josefa Antonia del Monte were both poets whose work voiced opposition to Spanish and Haitian agressions. The quote here from Josefa Antonia del Monte's poem reminds poet Josefa Antonia Perdomo (page 139, line 1) of her obligation to the campaign for national sovereignty and to the memory of her relative, Eugenio Perdomo, who was killed fighting annexation by Spain.

Page 141

Line 1: Salomé Ureña de Henríquez is regarded as one of the most important figures of Dominican letters. She was a poet, a feminist and an educator who fought for the intellectual emancipation of women and contributed significantly to political awareness in her time. She founded the Instituto de Señoritas in 1881.

Page 143

Line 22: María Nicolasa Billini was an educator from Baní, herself self-educated, and feminist who founded one of the first girl's schools, El Dominicano, in 1867.

Line 23: Anacaona Moscoso Puello was an educator in San Pedro de Macorís. She graduated from the Instituto de Señoritas and later became its director. She was also one of the founders of the Sociedad de Estudios Salomé Ureña.

Page 145
   Line 1: Antera Mota was an educator in Puerto Plata.

   Line 2: Rosa Sméster was an educator who studied medicine in France and fought for liberation during the U.S. military occupation.

   Line 6: Leonor Feltz was a pioneer educator who graduated from the Instituto de Señoritas.

   Line 7: Luisa Ozema Pellerano was an educator and revolutionary who fought against the U.S. intervention. She was also one of the founders of the Sociedad de Estudios Salomé Ureña.

   Lines 8 & 9: Ana Josefa Puello and Mercedes Laura Aguiar were educators and among the first graduates from the Instituto de Señoritas.

   Line 10: Abigaíl Mejía was a novelist and textbook writer who was dedicated to the emancipation of women. She founded the Club Nosotros and the Junta de Acción Feminista Dominicana to fight for the rights of professional women.

   Line 12: Evangelina Rodríguez was the first woman doctor in the Dominican Republic. She was openly critical of Trujillo.

Page 147
   Line 1: Flérida de Nolasco was a poet, folklorist, musicologist, literary critic, educator and historian of Dominican culture. She received the Premio Nacional for her cultural works.

Page 149
   Line 4: The U.S. ship Memphis was shipwrecked on August

18, 1916, on the coast near Santo Domingo. The irony of this event is that the 700 marines on the menacing warship were rescued by Dominican civilians. The women of the nearby towns made emergency bandages from their own clothing.

  Lines 12, 13 & 14: These lines are from the Dominican national anthem written by poet Emilio Prud'homme.

Page 151
  Line 15: Ceferina Calderón de Chávez contributed to the struggle against Spanish annexation by lending her horse and a guide to the Dominican troops.

Page 153
  Line 1: Trina (Trinidad) Moya de Vázquez was a Dominican poet who wrote school songs and the "Himno a las Madres," lines from which appear in the poem. She was the wife of Horacio Vázquez, President of the Republic after the withdrawal of U.S. troops in 1924.

Page 155
  Lines 6, 7 & 8: Fefita Justo Tavárez, Angela Ricart, Guillermina Puigsubirá, Estela Michel and María Faxas were mothers of revolutionaries killed. Fefita Justo Tavárez was the mother of revolutionary Manolo Tavárez Justo, leader of the 14th of June Clandestine Movement in 1959 and one of the guerrilleros killed in the ambush at La Manacla in December, 1963. He was the husband of Minerva Mirabal. Estela Michel was the mother of revolutionary Leonte Schott, killed in the ambush at La Manacla.

Page 159
  Line 1: Carmen Natalia was an important Dominican poet and novelist, a contemporary of Aída Cartagena Portalatín.

Line 15: Mercedes Mota was a militant feminist and educator.

Page 161
Line 3: The Substantive Law refers to the declaration of former President Juan Bosch which guaranteed that the Dominican Republic was a sovereign nation, independent of foreign influence. This law was suspended during the U.S. invasion of 1965 under the pretext of saving the lives of U.S. citizens.

Lines 15 & 16: These lines are from the Dominican national anthem written by poet Emilio Prud'homme.

BIBLIOGRAPHY

Works by Aída Cartagena Portalatín

Culturas africanas: rebeldes con causa. Santo Domingo: Editora Taller, 1986.

Danza, música e instrumentos de los indios de la Española. Santo Domingo: Editora Universidad Autónoma de Santo Domingo, 1974.

Del desconsuelo al compromiso. From Desolation to Compromise: A Bilingual Anthology of Poetry by Aída Cartagena Portalatín. Ed. Daisy Cocco de Filippis. Santo Domingo: Editora Taller, 1988.

Del sueño al mundo. Ciudad Trujillo: Ediciones La Poesía Sorprendida, 1945.

Dominican Poet Aída Cartagena Portalatín Reading From Her Work. (Sound Recording.) Santo Domingo: USIS, 1987.

Dos técnicas cerámicas indoantillanas: Diagnóstico del Orígen de los Yacimientos de las Antillas Mayores. Santo Domingo: Instituto Dominicano de Antropología, 197-.

En la casa del tiempo. Santo Domingo: Editora Universidad Autónoma de Santo Domingo, 1984.

Escalera para Electra. Santo Domingo: Editora Universidad Autónoma de Santo Domingo, 1970.

Estudio etnológico remanentes negros en el culto del Espíritu Santo de Villa Mella. Santo Domingo: Editora Universidad Autónoma de Santo Domingo, 1975.

José Vela Zanetti. Santo Domingo: Colección La Isla Necesaria, 1954.

La tarde en que murió Estafanía. Santo Domingo: Editora Taller, 1983.

La tierra escrita. Santo Domingo: Ediciones Brigadas Dominicanas, 1967.

Llámale verde. Ciudad Trujillo: Ediciones La Poesía Sorprendida, 1945.

Mi mundo el mar. Ciudad Trujillo: La Española, 1953.

Mujer y literatura. Homenaje a Aída Cartagena Portalatín. Ed. José Rafael Sosa. Santo Domingo: Editora Universitaria, 1986.

Narradores dominicanos. Ed. Aída Cartagena Portalatín. Caracas: Monte Avila Editores, 1969.

Tablero. Santo Domingo: Editora Taller, 1978.

Una mujer está sola. Ciudad Trujillo: La Española, 1955.

Una voz desatada. n.i., 1962.

Víspera del sueño, poemas para un atardecer. Ciudad Trujillo: Ediciones La Poesía Sorprendida, 1944.

Yania Tierra. Santo Domingo: Montesinos, 1981.

HISTORICAL REFERENCES

Arzeno, Julio. *Del folk-lore musical dominicano.* Santo Domingo: Roques Román Hnos., 1927.

Báez Díaz, Tomás. *La mujer dominicana.* Santo Domingo: Editora Educativa Dominicana, 1980.

Bell, Ian. *The Dominican Republic.* Boulder: Westview Press, 1981.

Calder, Bruce J. *The Impact of Intervention.* Austin: University of Texas Press, 1984.

de las Casas, Bartolomé. *Historia de las Indias.* México, D.F.: Fondo de Cultura Económica, 1951.

Colón, Cristóbal. *Los cuatro viajes del almirante y su testimonio.* Madrid: Espasa-Calpe, 1971.

Cordero, Margarita. *Mujeres de abril.* Santo Domingo: CIPAF, 1985.

Crassweller, Robert D. *Trujillo: The Life and Times of a Caribbean Dictator.* New york: The Macmillan Co., 1966.

Cuello, H,. José Israel. *¿Qué era la resistencia antitrujillista interna a la hora de la invasión de Constanza, Maimón y Esero Hondo, el de junio de 1959?* Santo Domingo: Fundación Testimonio, 1983.

Duarte, Rosa. *Apuntes de Rosa Duarte.* Santo Domingo: Editora del Caribe, 1970.

Ferreras, Ramón Alberto. *Historia del feminismo en la República*

Dominicana. Santo Domingo: Editorial del Nordeste, 1991.

Fuentes, Matons, Laureano. *Las artes en Santiago de Cuba*. La Habana: Letras Cubanas, 1981.

Galeano, Eduardo. *Las venas abiertas de América Latina*. México: Siglo XXI, 1971.

———. *Open Veins of Latin America*. New York: Monthly Review Press, 1973.

Galván, Manuel de Jesús. *The Cross and the Sword*. Trans. Robert Graves. Bloomington: Indiana University Press, 1954.

———. *Enriquillo*. Santo Domingo: Editora Taller, 1975.

García, José Gabriel. *Rasgos biográficos de dominicanos célebres*. Santo Domingo: Editora del Caribe, 1971.

Gleijeses, Piero. *The Dominican Crisis*. Baltimore: The Johns Hopkins University Press, 1978.

Grimaldi, Victor. *Entrevistas — análisis — reportajes*. Santo Domingo: Editora Cosms, 1977.

Henríquez Ureña, Max. *Los yanquis en Santo Domingo*. Madrid: Aguilar, 1929.

Horowitz, Irving Louis, Josué de Castro and John Gerassi, eds. *Latin American Radicalism*. New York: Vantage Books, 1969.

Logan, Rayford W. *Haiti and the Dominican Republic*. New York and London: oxford University Press, 1968.

Loven, Sven. *Origins of the Tainan Culture*. Gotebrg: Elanders, 1935.

de Marchena, Enrique. *Del areito de Anacaona al poema folklórico*. Ciudad Trujillo: Editora Montalvo, 1942.

Martin, John Bartlow. *Ovetaken By Events*. Garden City: Doubleday & Company, 1966.

Moreno, José A. *Barrios in Arms*. Pittsburgh: University of Pittsburgh Press, 1970.

Moya Pons, Frank. *Historia colonial de Santo Domingo*. Santiago, República Dominicana: Universidad Católica Madre y Maestra, 1976.

Olivier, Maritza. *Cinco siglos con la mujer dominicana*. Santo Domingo: Amigo del Hogar, 1975.

Peña Castillo, Domingo A. *Memorias de un revolucionario*. Santo Domingo: Editora Alfa y Omega, 1983.

Rouse, Irving. *The Tainos*. New Haven: Yale University Press, 1992.

Slater, Jerome. *Intervention and Negotiation*. New York: Harper & Row, 1970.

Wilson, Samuel M. *Hispaniola: Caribbean Chiefdoms in the Age of Columbus*. Tuscaloosa: The University of Alabama Press, 1990.